Hezekiah Butterworth

Zigzag journeys in classic lands

Tommy Toby's trip to Mount Parnassus

Hezekiah Butterworth

Zigzag journeys in classic lands
Tommy Toby's trip to Mount Parnassus

ISBN/EAN: 9783744744638

Printed in Europe, USA, Canada, Australia, Japan

Cover: Foto ©Andreas Hilbeck / pixelio.de

More available books at **www.hansebooks.com**

ZIGZAG JOURNEYS

IN

CLASSIC LANDS;

OR,

TOMMY TOBY'S TRIP TO MOUNT PARNASSUS.

BY

HEZEKIAH BUTTERWORTH,
AUTHOR OF "ZIGZAG JOURNEYS IN EUROPE."

BOSTON:
ESTES AND LAURIAT.
1881.

PREFACE.

HE warm welcome which the public gave to "ZIG-ZAG JOURNEYS IN EUROPE," and its large sale and continued success have led the publishers and the writer to plan a series of entertaining and instructive books which shall illustrate the scenery, manners and customs, history and legendary lore of different parts of the world.

It was decided that the second volume should be such as would tend to awaken an interest in classical studies, and afford a glimpse of the past glory and a view of the present condition of Greece and Rome. The tourists were to pass through the old Roman empire and to go over the waters crossed by Ulysses, Æneas, the Apostle Paul, and by the early arts in their progress towards the West.

The former volume met with so much acceptance as a holiday gift-book that a special Christmas chapter has been prepared for this, describing one of the entertainments and relating some of the best stories of the Zigzag Club.

The writer is indebted to Mrs. MARIE B. WILLIAMS of Opelousas, La., for the admirable story of De Soto, many of the facts of which are translated from a choice Portuguese work.

A profuse use of illustrations and curious and humorous stories is a part of the plan of this series of books. It is intended that these popular features shall be helps towards forming the best literary tastes for wholesome reading, and so lead to the profitable companionship of the best books.

Should the present volume be as kindly received as the first, it is intended to follow it by " Zigzag Journeys in the Orient," which shall take the young tourists down the Danube, across the Black and Caspian Seas, and up the Volga, giving a view of the romantic histories that are associated with these water-courses of the storied Empires of the East.

28 WORCESTER STREET,
BOSTON, MASS.

To the Memory

OF

WILLIE ALBERT TOWLE,

A LATE MEMBER OF THE BOSTON LATIN SCHOOL,

WHO TOOK A HELPFUL INTEREST IN THE PREPARATION OF THE WORK,

THIS VOLUME IS AFFECTIONATELY DEDICATED.

CHAPTER	PAGE
I. THE ZIGZAG CLUB	15
II. THE ZIGZAG CLUB'S CHRISTMAS STORIES	29
III. A NEW JOURNEY PROPOSED	63
IV. FROM BOSTON TO LISBON	81
V. FROM LISBON TO GRANADA	106
VI. THROUGH THE HEART OF SPAIN	128
VII. MARSEILLES AND THE RHONE	157
VIII. GENOA, MILAN, AND VENICE	190
IX. PARNASSUS	201
X. THE LANDS OF VULCAN AND CYCLOPS	232
XI. ROME	266

ILLUSTRATIONS.

	PAGE
Peter the Great and Little Louis XV.	Frontispiece.
Climbing Parnassus	Half-title
Nix's Mate	16
"I've seen a Spoke!"	20
"What a Mistake!"	21
Basin of Neptune	23
Statues in the grounds of Versailles	25
Fountains at Versailles	26
The Grand Monarch	27
The Magic Raisins	31
The Pinakothek	33
Bavarian Market-people	34
Market-place, Nuremburg	35
The Glyptothek	37
Outgeneralled by a Gander	38
Goatherd's Hut	39
Bavarian Peasants	41
The Irish Giant	44
Defile in the Hartz Mountains	49
In the Hartz Mountains	51
Supposed Spectres	55
Alfred the Great watching the Peasant's Loaves	59
The Shores of the Mediterranean	65
Ruins of the Parthenon	69
Italian Beggars	73
Italian Mountebanks	74
The Roman Forum	75
Beggars in Rome	77
Venice	79
Columbus looking for Land	83

	PAGE
Columbus in Prison	87
Bivouac of De Soto's Expedition in Florida	91
Burial of De Soto	95
Crater of Volcano	99
Milking a Goat	103
Swinging	104
Travelling in Spain	107
The Tower of Belem	109
Doorway of Santa Maria, Belem	111
Gate of the Castle of Pintra de Cintra	113
Tableaux of "The Cid" in the Middle Ages	115
Interior of the Cathedral, Seville	119
Hall of the Ambassadors, Seville	123
Court of the Lions	129
Fountain in the Alhambra	132
General View of the Alhambra	133
Cave-dwelling of the Gypsies	137
An old Gypsy	139
Bull-fight	141
The Royal Palace, Madrid	145
The Escurial	149
The Leaning Tower of Saragossa	153
Public Garden, Marseilles	159
Girondists singing the Marseillaise Hymn	163
Château of the Popes, Avignon	165
Cathedral of Lyons	166
Park of the Tête d'Or, Lyons	167
Fountain in the Park of la Tête d'Or	169
Christianity established in Gaul	170
Mounted Gauls	171

ILLUSTRATIONS.

	PAGE
Gauls subjugated by the Romans	173
Belzunce amidst the Plague-stricken	175
Preaching the Crusade	179
Crusaders on the way to Palestine	183
Pierre	185
Jacques	186
"You are a Liar and a Villain!"	188
Donkeys	191
Genoese	192
On the Canal	196
Venetian Water-carrier	198
The Dwarf of Lombardy	199
The Temple of Apollo	201
The Propylæa	204
View of Athens from the Acropolis	205
Temple of the Wingless Victory	208
Theatre of Herod	209
The Council of the Gods	212
Plain of Troy	213
Helen and Priam on the Ramparts	214
Funeral Pile of Patroclus	215
Blinding of the Cyclops	216
Escape of Ulysses	217
Ulysses recognized by Eurycleia	218
The Temple of Zeus, Olympia	220
Modern Festival at the Temple of Jupiter	227
Messina	232
Waves of Volcanic Fire	235
Mt. Ætna	238
Lava Beds of Mt. Ætna	239
The Headland of Cape d'Alessio	240
Cathedral of Palermo	241
Taormina	243
West Porch of the Cathedral, Palermo	244
Lava Streams	245
South Porch of the Cathedral, Palermo	247
Aci Castello	248
The Cathedral of Monreale	250
Western Porch, Cathedral of Monreale	251
Cloisters of the Cathedral of Monreale	253
The Palace of La Ziza	254
Edith discovers the body of Harold	259
Archbishop Aldred's Curse	261
Street-scene in Naples	263
A Military Officer	264
A Beggar without Legs	265
The Arena of the Colosseum	269
Erythræan Sibyl, Sistine Chapel	273
Interior of the Colosseum	277
Ancient Constantinian Basilica of St. Peter's	281
Ruins of the Palace of Tiberius	284
Arch of Constantine	285
Arch of Septimius Severus	289
View from the Palatine	293
Fountain of Trevi	297
Piazza and Garden in Rome	301
Caldarium of the Baths of Caracalla	305
Prayer	307
Peasant Family in Rome	308
A Roman Villa	309
The German Artist	311
An Enthusiastic Copyist	312
The Moses of Michael Angelo	313
Adieu	318

ZIGZAG JOURNEYS IN CLASSIC LANDS.

CLIMBING PARNASSUS.

ZIGZAG JOURNEYS IN CLASSIC LANDS.

CHAPTER I.

THE ZIGZAG CLUB.

M. TOEPFER. — THE RETURN FROM EUROPE. — BOSTON HARBOR. — NIX'S MATE. — MRS. TRAVIS'S PARROT. — THE CUSTOM-HOUSE OFFICER. — "WHEN I WAS IN EUROPE." — "HE IS AN AMERICAN."

A DELIGHTFUL schoolmaster was M. Toepfer, and when he died he left behind a fragrant memory in the homes and schools of France. He used to wander with his classes during the vacations of summer over the Alps and the Oberland, and into the green valleys of France and Italy, telling stories as he went, and publishing his stories and adventures for the entertainment of young people who could not make such free-and-easy excursions. He and his classes had no fixed route in their travels, but went wherever a picturesque scene, an historic ruin, or a pleasing tradition, attracted them. His midsummer wanderings in this hap-hazard way he called "Zigzag Journeys," and the French school-boy was usually pleased to receive the splendidly illustrated volumes for his reward of merit, or Christmas or holiday present.

In a former volume, entitled " Zigzag Journeys in Europe," we have told how an American school became interested in the good French teacher's plan of securing for his pupils both recreation and historical instruction during the midsummer vacation; how a class arranged to visit Europe with their teacher; what adventures it met and what scenes of historic stories and legends it visited.

We related how the school formed a society called "The Zigzag Club," for the purpose of gaining as much information as possible about the lands which the class proposed to visit; and how, at the meetings of the Club, historic stories and legends of particular countries and localities were told.

We should further repeat that the teacher was Master Lewis; that the class which went abroad with him consisted of six boys,— Frank Gray, Ernest Wynn, Wyllys Wynn, "Tommy" Toby, George Howe, and Leander Towle; that the class visited Scotland, England, Belgium, Normandy, and Brittany; that two of the boys made the excursion in the most economical way by which it would be possible for a student to visit these countries, and remained abroad but a short time; and that the others zigzagged through these delightful countries at leisure, and studied history, poetry, and legendary lore.

On the voyage going out, the class had suffered from sea-sickness. The return was over a calm sea, and Master Lewis took this favourable time to explain to the boys the physical geography of the ocean, and the wonders of sub-marine life. Nine calm days brought them in sight of Boston Harbor.

"It is delightful to be in a ship going out," said Wyllys Wynn, as a great ocean steamer passed by on the calm September afternoon.

NIX'S MATE.

"It is more delightful to be in a ship coming in," said Tommy Toby. "Yonder is Nix's Mate."

"Who was Nix?" asked Wyllys of Master Lewis.

"He was the captain of a ship in old colonial times. His mate was supposed to have murdered him, and he was buried on this island. The mate was arrested, and convicted of the murder on circumstantial evidence, and was sentenced to be hung on the island. The island was as green then as it is black now. The man was hung near where the black pyramid now stands.

"The mate declared that he was innocent of the murder. He believed Providence would witness his innocence after his death. He said: —

"'I prophesy that this green will become a desolate spot. The ocean will wash away the place where I shall perish, and that shall be the sign in the future by which all shall know that I am innocent of the charge against me.'

"The green vegetation slowly disappeared from the island; then the island itself wasted away, and the rocks on which it had been turned black, and only the dark pyramid erected as a warning to ships, and a few sharp crags, now remain.

"'The island is gone,
And the mate is free
Of this cruel charge
Made by history.'

"So runs the old song. The event took place about two hundred years ago. Another hundred years will perhaps witness the disappearance of the last rock of the island.

"I tell the story," continued Master Lewis, "not that I have full confidence that the island is disappearing for the reason assigned, but to show you that our own shores are rich in stories as well as those we have been visiting."

"Do you wish to know which is the most glorious dome I have seen during the last three months?" asked Tommy. He pointed.

The golden dome of the State House was shining in the sun. He added, —

"It may not represent art, but it represents liberty, and America is the best land I ever was"—

"Born in, — to be perfectly truthful," said Master Lewis. "One ought to be modest in speaking of one's own country."

Some curious incidents had happened during the homeward voyage, which ended in an amusing episode when the ship arrived, and the custom-house officers came on board.

Several times, during the pleasant days, a finely dressed lady had greeted Master Lewis, in the morning, with a monologue which became noticeable for its sameness.

"Good mauning, Mr. Lewis. A re-markably fine mauning, this mauning. I hope you are well, Mr. Lewis.

"Do you think we will be likely to arrive at mauning or at night, Mr. Lewis.

"*Will we be likely to be detained long?* I hope we will not be detained long, Mr. Lewis."

When this had been repeated for several mornings in the hearing of the boys, Tommy Toby said to Master Lewis, —

"What does the lady mean by 'Will we be likely to be detained long?'"

"She probably has dutiable goods in her trunk or about her person," replied Master Lewis, "and hopes to arrive in port at night, that she may more easily evade the custom-house officers."

"She would seem to be too much of a lady for such a plan as that," said Tommy.

"The tricks and deceptions which fine ladies use to evade the custom-house officers, and to get the goods they have purchased abroad into port free of duty, is one of the most discreditable exhibitions one meets in travelling," continued Master Lewis. "Many people, both women and men, seem to consider it smart to be untruthful to a custom-house officer. Now a lie is a lie, and a deception is a lie in any situation. It requires a remarkably strong character to pass through the custom-house inspection, and maintain a true self-respect. I have known ladies to conceal point-lace in their hair, jewels in apples and oranges, and to wear fur capes in the hottest days in summer, to escape the payment of duties."

"Are not men as dishonest as women in this respect?" asked Tommy.

"Yes," said Master Lewis. "Why I speak of women is because women generally have a finer moral sense, and more conscientious self-respect, than men. The finer the character, the more painful seems the departure from the strict practice of truth."

The lady's name was Travis. She had a great amount of baggage, and a poodle dog, and a parrot beside. The parrot was frequently taken into the saloon and on deck, where it greatly amused the passengers.

The bird could speak several words very distinctly, but its most wonderful accomplishment was the utterance of two whole sentences. These were, —

"You get out! I shall die."

Sometimes it added to these the exclamations, "Oh! Oh! Oh."

When Polly became tired of a visitor to her cage, or became vexed by being too much talked to, she would say, —

"You get out! I shall die."

As Polly was disposed to scream, "I shall die. Oh! Oh! Oh!" whenever the ship gave a lurch or pitched perceptibly, Mrs. Travis sometimes put the bird in a small unoccupied apartment amidships, which she had received permission to do from an officer.

A French lad employed on the ship thought one day that this unoccupied apartment would be a better sleeping-room than his berth, and received permission to make a bed there. He knew nothing of Mrs. Travis's habit of taking Polly, when she was too noisy, to the banishment of the room.

The lad one night took a candle and went to the room. He had partly undressed, when he heard a dreadful voice, which he thought to be supernatural, say, —

"You get out!"

He obeyed the admonition at once, his hair standing on end, and was presently found by an officer, who said sharply, —

"What are you wandering about with a light for?"

"I've seen a *spoke*," said the lad, bewildered. "Will you go back with me, and get my clothes?"

The man and boy turned back to the room.

As the officer entered, there came as from the air a more vigorous expostulation, —

"You get out! I shall die. Oh! Oh! Oh!"

But the officer understood the matter, and the story passed from mouth to mouth on the following day.

When the custom-house officer came to examine Mrs. Travis's trunk, the lady passed backward and forward on the deck in a very cool, dignified way, after saying carelessly to him, —

"It must be very annoying to search a lady's trunk at a time like this, when every one is so impatient to get on shore."

"I'VE SEEN A SPOKE!"

But the officer did not seem to be in any haste: he carefully turned over parcel after parcel.

As the examination proceeded, and the bottom of the chest was nearly reached, Mrs. Travis lost her assumed dignity, and tiptoed up behind the conscientious official, and gazed with staring eyes over his shoulder.

The officer took from the chest a suspicious-looking bundle. On it was a written direction, —

"*Mary*, when you open the trunk, see that these clothes are mended before they are put away."

This looked innocent, certainly. The bundle was tied up with cords, and there were hard knots at all the angles.

"I hope you will tie up the bundle securely again," said Mrs. Travis, evidently hoping it would not be untied.

The officer looked at the knots, then coolly took his pocket-knife and made perfectly easy work in laying open the bundle.

"Are these the clothes that you wish 'Mary' to mend?" he said coolly.

The bundle contained several silk dress-patterns *uncut*.

"What a mistake!" said Mrs. Travis. "I must have marked the *wrong* things. Those are some goods that I bought for my own private use."

"WHAT A MISTAKE!"

"They are dutiable," said the officer.

"Dutiable! my own things! Oh!"

Polly caught sound of the "Oh," and knew her mistress was in trouble. Her cage was close to the trunk, at the end, and partly out of sight.

Polly screamed, "Oh!"

The exclamation seemed to proceed from the trunk. The officer started.

"You get out!"

The officer rose to his feet.

"You get out!"

"I think I will," said the gentleman, discovering the cause of the mystery. "I am very sorry, very sorry, but I shall have to take this bundle with me; very sorry; good-evening, madam."

"I shall die!" screamed Polly.

And poor Mrs. Travis's look was as despairing as Polly's melancholy words.

The boys' excursion to Europe stimulated them in their studies, gave them a fresh relish for the best reading, and led them to take more intelligent and broader views of the duties of life. But it made several of them a little pedantic. Frank Gray, especially, was heard referring to "the time when I was in Europe," on almost every occasion; and he always tried to make it appear that every thing he saw in Europe was immensely superior to any thing that could be seen at home.

George Howe was a practical, clear-sighted boy; and he had little sympathy with Frank's assuming airs over the magnificent sights he had seen in Europe.

Several of the boys of the academy were walking on the Common in Boston one fine autumn day, and among them was Frank, still dazzled by the splendours of Europe. The fountains were playing under the trees, and over the grand old elms, on Beacon Street Mall, the dome of the State House was shining, looking very modest in Frank's eyes after his recent visit to English and French cathedrals and palaces.

"The fountain in the Frog Pond is playing," said George Howe. "Let us go down there and see it; how it tosses its spray over the trees into the light of the sun!"

"The Frog Pond!" said Frank, in a tone of depreciation, "*when I was in Europe* I saw the Basin of Neptune at the Palace of Versailles."

BASIN OF NEPTUNE.

"And so did I," said George, "but I am just as glad to see the good old Frog Pond as I was before I went to Europe."

"All the air seemed full of fountains at Versailles," continued Frank, to one of the new scholars, "and you cannot fancy the beauty of the bowers, grottoes, statues, and works of art that rise on every

STATUES IN THE GROUNDS OF VERSAILLES.

hand. It is said that two hundred millions of dollars were spent upon the palace and park, and that an army of Frenchmen were employed for years upon the palace."

"At a time when the people had no more political rights and privileges than horses," said George; "and when the poor man's table consisted of two or three dishes, and often of more dishes than kinds of food."

"But just think of it," said Frank, "two hundred millions of dollars! What should we think of a public building that cost forty millions of dollars?"

FOUNTAINS AT VERSAILLES.

"I should think it a piece of very great extravagance," said George, "and a matter of great wickedness and folly, if it were built by spilling the blood of poor people in unnecessary wars, and overtaxing their hard earnings in short intervals of peace. *That* is the way Versailles was built, and my head was not at all turned by my short visit to all of its magnificence. Louis XIV. — the Grand Monarch — left

THE GRAND MONARCH.

the nation eight hundred million dollars in debt. Only think of *that!* It used to take, at one time, thirty million dollars a year to meet his expenses; and that was when several of the great palaces we saw were building, and when the peasants were so taxed that they had scarcity of shoes and outward covering. What do you think of *that?* He was succeeded by Louis XV. The young king was told that all the people of France belonged to him, and he believed that he owned them in the same sense that one owns a herd of cattle. Peter the Great, on visiting France, kissed the boy with delight, as a brother with him in the inheritance of nations. During the whole reign of Louis XV. wicked women influenced the king in all things, and so ruled France. People were arrested for offending any member of his dissipated court, on secret warrants called *lettres de cachet.* They were thrown without any form of trial into the dungeons of the Bastile and other prisons, to rot alive. A joke at the expense of Madame de Pompadour is said to have led to the seven years' war. If even a rich man remonstrated against taxation, he might be arrested on one of these *lettres de cachet,* and dropped into one of the *oubliettes,* or stone jugs, of the Bastile to suffer and die forgotten. One hundred and fifty thousand of these *lettres de cachet* were issued during the reign of Louis XV. alone. A young collegian made a sarcastic rhyme about the king, and was immured without trial in the Bastile thirty years. What do you think of *that?*"

"I think you are an American," said Tommy.

The boys laughed, and heartily joined in the chorus of a song which Tommy began: —

> " For he himself hath said it,
> And 't is greatly to his credit,
> That he is an American;
> For he might have been a Russian,
> A Frenchman, Turk, or Prussian,
> Or perhaps Italian;
> But, in spite of all temptation
> To belong to other nation,
> He remains an American."

CHAPTER II.

THE ZIGZAG CLUB'S CHRISTMAS STORIES.

THE CHRISTMAS PARTY. — CHRISTMAS MÉLANGE. — PUZZLES. — STORY OF THE KING WHO WAS OUTGENERALLED BY A GANDER. — STORY OF KING FREDERICK WILLIAM AND THE IRISH GIANT. — STORY OF THE JOLLY OLD ABBOT OF CANTERBURY. — STORY OF THE LITTLE OLD MAN OF THE FOREST. — STORY OF THE TANNER OF TAMWORTH. — STORY OF PROCOPIUS AND THE CHILDREN.

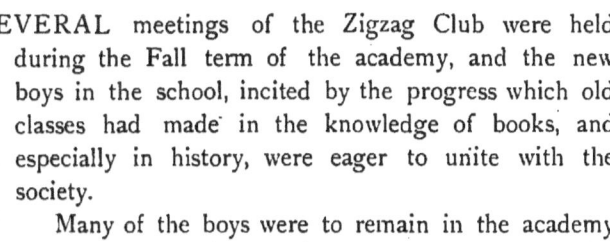

SEVERAL meetings of the Zigzag Club were held during the Fall term of the academy, and the new boys in the school, incited by the progress which old classes had made in the knowledge of books, and especially in history, were eager to unite with the society.

Many of the boys were to remain in the academy town during the winter holidays; and some three weeks before the Christmas season Master Lewis invited the class that had been abroad, and all the other members of the Club who were not intending to return to their homes, to spend Christmas evening in his rooms.

"It will give me much pleasure to entertain you," he said. "You might also, if you chose, agreeably contribute to the entertainment by arranging for it sports, games, charades, or, better still, by telling old-time Christmas stories, or relating any pleasant incidents in keeping with the occasion."

At the next meeting of the Club, a programme was arranged for an entertainment by the boys at Master Lewis's on Christmas evening. It was as follows: —

CHRISTMAS MÉLANGE.

1. CAROL . . . . *Adeste Fideles*.
   BY THE CLUB.
2. CHARADE . . . . *Charlotte Russe*.
   In four acts, the dialogue to be *impromptu*.
3. HUMOROUS STORY . . . . *Outgeneralled by a Gander*.
   THOMAS TOBY.
4. HUMOROUS STORY . . . . *The Irish Giant*.
   FRANK GRAY.
5. HUMOROUS STORY . . . . *King John and the Abbot of Canterbury*.
   ERNEST WYNN.
6. A MYSTERIOUS STORY . . . . *The Little Old Man of the Forest*.
   PROMISED BY MR. LEWIS.
7. SONG . . . . *The Golden Carol*.
   WYLLYS WYNN.
8. HUMOROUS STORY . . . . *The Tanner of Tamworth*.
   GEORGE HOWE.
9. POEM . . . . *Procopius and the Children*.
   WYLLYS WYNN.
10. CHARADE . . . . *Good Night*.
    The dialogue to be *impromptu*.

Several of the new scholars promised to take part in the exercises, by relating humorous anecdotes, should there be time for a more extended programme.

The Club met at Master Lewis's on the afternoon before the entertainment, and were served with an old-fashioned Christmas dinner at five o'clock. The tables were set under gas-jets which were so intermingled among boughs of evergreen, which completely covered the chandeliers, as to produce a very picturesque effect. When the dessert was brought in, each plate contained, besides nuts and raisins, a pleasing Christmas gift.

After the meal, and while the Club was yet seated at the table, Tommy Toby performed some little feats in legerdemain, which proved interesting. As perhaps some readers may have received this volume as a holiday present, we will tell how Tommy's best trick, on this occasion, may be performed: —

He took four raisins from the dessert-dish and placed them about a foot apart on the table, so as to indicate a square. He folded a couple of table-napkins about four or five times, so as to form pads about five inches square. He took one of these in the manner indicated in the illustration. The fingers are under the pad.

He informed the company that these were magic raisins, and possessed some very striking qualities. For instance, he proposed to leave it for the company to judge whether they did not presently pass through the table. In the course of his remarks he brought down the two napkins carelessly over the raisins on the farther row.  He left the right-hand napkin on the table, but, in withdrawing the hand, brought away the raisin between the second and third fingers, at the same time saying, —

"You must notice how many raisins I place under each napkin."

He lifted the left-hand napkin, as if to show that there was only one raisin beneath it, and transferred it to the palm of the right hand, behind which the raisin was concealed.

He replaced the folded napkin on the raisin, and in doing so left the concealed raisin beside it. He took up the third raisin, put it under the table, and concealed it between his fingers. He said "Pass." He picked up the napkin on the table, and *two* raisins were found beneath, the appearance being that the raisin in the right hand passed through the table.

He had now a raisin still concealed in the right hand between the fingers. He transferred the napkin to the right hand, and placed it over raisins number 1 and 2, leaving number 3 beside them. He took up raisin number 4, saying "Pass," lifted the napkin, and under it *three* raisins were found.

Another Christmas diversion, which Tommy introduced after dinner, may also interest the reader. He exhibited a small card, called, for the sake of exciting curiosity, a magic card. It was covered with five rows of letters. We will explain the puzzle, and illustrate how the letters may be made to reveal one's thoughts.

A	B	D	H	P	
C	C	E	I		
E	F	F	J		
G	G	G	K		
I	J	L	L		
K	K	M	M		
M	N	N	N		
O	O	O	O		
Q	R	T	X	Q	
S	S	U	Y	R	
U	V	V	Z	S	
W	W	W		T	
Y	Z			U	
				V	
				W	
				X	
				Y	
				Z	

Say to your friend: "Think of a word. Do not tell me what it is. Answer my questions, and I will tell you what it is.

"In what column is the first letter of the word you have thought of found?"

If it be found in but one column, it is the top letter; if it occurs in more than one, it is found by adding the alphabetical numbers of the top letters of these columns, A representing 1, B 2, D 4, etc., and their sum will be the number of the letter sought. For example: Your friend thinks of the word JANE. J is found in two columns commencing with B and H; B = 2 and H = 8; 8 + 2 = 10. J is the tenth letter of the alphabet. The second letter will be found in but one column and will be A, etc.

The evening entertainment opened at seven. The Club sang finely Novello's arrangement of the ancient Latin hymn, "Adeste Fideles."

"Adeste, Fideles,
Læti triumphantes,
Venite, venite in Bethlehem,
Natum videte
Regem angelorum,
Venite adoremus,
Venite adoremus,
Venite adoremus,
Dominum."

The charade consisted of four short dialogues, with tableaux representing the *Shah* of Persia, *Lot* fleeing from Sodom, a *Ruse* to get rid of an unwelcome visitor, and a party at a table eating *Charlotte-Russe*. Not one of the company not in the secret was able to guess the word.

TOMMY TOBY'S STORY.
OUTGENERALLED BY A GANDER.

You have heard of Munich and its works of art; its Pinakothek, or wonderful house of pictures; its Glyptothek, or museum of sculpture; its palace crowded with every object that can delight the eye. Munich is the capital of Bavaria.

THE PINAKOTHEK.

You have read of the fine old city of Nuremberg, with its high walls and rocky châteaux and castles. It is said still to resemble a town of the Middle Ages. Nuremberg is in Franconia, and Franconia is in Bavaria.

One of the industries of Bavaria is raising geese. You may find people with geese to sell in the Bavarian market-places, and may sometimes see at a fair the odd sight of a peasant woman with a live goose under her arm, awaiting a purchaser for the distressed-looking bird.

These geese are raised in the valleys, and a boy is employed by the season to watch a large flock of geese, as a shepherd in the hill country is accustomed to watch sheep, or as a goatherd, who often lives in some rocky hut he has made in the mountains, is employed to watch goats.

One summer day Maximilian Joseph, the King of Bavaria, sat reading, in plain citizen's dress, in the delicious shadows of the royal park. The heat was severe, and the atmosphere was hazy and dreamy, and possibly the book that the good king was reading was a dull one, for he fell asleep. On waking, he determined to drive away further drowsiness by taking a walk.

BAVARIAN MARKET PEOPLE.

He came to a sunny meadow, barred with long shadows of trees, which sloped down to a large pond. When he came to the margin of the pond, he remembered that he had left his book behind. He would be sorry to lose the book, but he did not wish to go back after it, so he looked around for some one to send. He presently espied a tall, lank, ignorant-looking boy, taking care of a flock of geese.

He called the boy to him.

"On a bench under a great ash in the park you will find a book. Go and bring it to me, and I will give you a florin."

The boy did not know the king. But he knew that strolling people were not apt to offer florins for slight services.

"Do you take me for a fool?" asked he.

"What makes you think I am joking?" asked the king.

"Because money does not come so easy as that. You must be one of the gentlemen from the castle."

MARKET PLACE, NUREMBERG.

"Well, what of that? Here is the florin. Go for the book."

The boy's eyes sparkled. The money was almost as much as he received for taking care of a flock of geese for a season. Yet he hesitated.

"Well!" said the king. "Why don't you go?"

The boy took off his hat, and rubbed the side of his head.

"I would if I could; but the geese?"

"You little dolt! I will take care of the geese."

"*You!*" exclaimed the boy. " You do not look as though you knew enough. If they fly through the fields while I am gone, I shall have the damage to pay, and may lose my place, and then I would be ruined entirely. You see that one with a black head? It is a sly bird, and will be sure to lead the flock astray while I am gone."

The king smiled.

THE GLYPTOTHEK.

"I know how to manage men, and I think I can manage a *goose.*"

He bade the boy go at once. The latter hesitated, but finally consented, giving the king a whip to crack in case the geese should begin to disperse.

But the winged subjects of the monarch soon perceived that their master was gone, and began to cackle and announce the news to each other most jubilantly. The black-headed bird began to march and countermarch, and the whole flock under his able generalship scattered, each separating from the other, and forming a line which grew longer and longer. The king issued his commands in a loud voice, and tried to crack the whip, but all his efforts went for nothing. The geese obeyed the orders of the gander.

OUTGENERALLED BY A GANDER.

The king ran hither and thither, but the line of the geese only grew longer and more diverse.

GOATHERD'S HUT.

THE ZIGZAG CLUB'S CHRISTMAS STORIES. 41

"Shew!" said the king. It was the only goose language he knew.

"Honk!" said the gander, and the geese obeyed the mysterious command, and made their line longer and longer.

At last the "black-headed bird" gave a triumphant "Honk, Honk," and the whole column of geese rose into the air and flew into the fields. The king, bathed in perspiration, sat down in great vexation to find that his royal authority was of so little account in the goose kingdom.

BAVARIAN PEASANTS.

Presently the boy returned, and saw what had happened. He was in great terror and distress.

"Did I not tell you that you did not know enough to take care of geese? Now you must help me find them again!"

The king consented, and late in the day the flock was gathered.

"I'll never go away again," said the boy; "not for the king himself."

The king returned to the castle quite thoughtful. It was easier, after all, to manage a kingdom than to outgeneral an old gander,— a consideration that was hardly flattering to kingly dignity.

FRANK GRAY'S STORY.
KING FREDERICK AND THE IRISH GIANT.

A queer and testy man was Frederick William I., the second king of Prussia, and the father of the renowned monarch, Frederick the Great. He ascended the throne in 1713.

He assembled and drilled a great army in time of peace. He was very proud of their numbers and discipline, and among his queer ambitions was one that was very odd indeed. He desired to have a certain corps of soldiers that should consist wholly of giants.

So he sent his agents all over Europe giant-hunting.

A difficult task the agents had, for giants were not so numerous in Europe as they are supposed to have been in very ancient times, before history was written. But one of them met with good fortune, as you shall presently be told.

One day, as one of the Prussian recruiting-sergeants was visiting London in search of tall men for Frederick's service, his attention was called to a crowd in the streets.

He entered the crowd curiously, and to his amazement and delight he there found on exhibition the tallest man he had ever seen.

The man was an Irish giant. His head was covered with thick yellow hair; his shoulders were broad. He rose above the crowd like a tower among houses.

He had come to England to seek work. He was now out of money, but he was still good-natured and merry. Fat people usually are cheerful, whatever may be their condition.

The recruiting-sergeant elbowed his way through the crowd, greatly excited thus to find the very man he had been so diligently looking for.

He laid his hand on the Irishman's sleeve.

"Come with me, come with me! I'm a soldier myself, and I am always ready to help a comrade in distress."

"But Oi'm not a soldier."

"Aren't you? Why, you look like every inch a soldier; any man would take you for one. You ought to be a soldier, sure. But never mind that. Come and dine with me."

"That I will," said Pat, "and ye need not be after axing me twice."

The Irishman's appetite was as great as his body, and when he was well filled with a liberal meal, he was always credulous and jolly and easy to be persuaded.

"You are a fine fellow," said the sergeant; "a wonderfully fine fellow. Did you never think of turning soldier?"

"An' what should I turn soldier for?"

"For honour and glory."

"A cannon ball would n't be apt to *miss* me, sure; and what good would honour and glory do me, when my head was gone, clane gone intirely?"

"For money."

"How much?"

"I will offer you a safe position in the Prussian life-guards. The king, I am sure, would pay four hundred pounds down for a strapping fellow like you."

"Four hundred pounds! Four hundred pounds! Do I hear my own ears? Faix, I will not be long in choosing. Pat O'Flannigan is the boy for yez."

"Good. Can you speak German?"

"German, is it? Dutch-like? sorra a word of German can I spake, if it were to save my life from the hangman."

"Well, no matter. Three sentences are all you need to know. I can teach you them."

"What be thez?"

"When the king first sees you in the ranks he will come to you and say,—

"'How old are you?'"

"An' what shall I say?"

"'Twenty-seven years.'"

"Then he will ask you how long you have been in the service."

"An' what will I say thin?"

"'Three weeks.'"

"Then he will say,—

"'Are you provided with clothes and rations,' and you will answer,—

"'Both.'"

"I think my head will hold that much."

"I will try you. How old are you?"

"Twenty-seven years."

"How long have you been in the service?"

"Three weeks."

"Are you provided with clothes and rations?"

"Both."

On the journey to Berlin the sergeant asked the happy recruit these questions daily. He answered promptly and correctly.

About three weeks after his arrival, he appeared on parade in the corps of giants for the first time. There were Arabs and Danes, and Moors and Swedes in the brigade; giants from almost all the countries of Europe, — but Pat stood like a Saul among them all.

The king saw him, and his face shone.

He beckoned to him to step forward.

Pat stepped forward proudly, and presented arms.

"I have n't seen you before," said the king. "How long have you been in the service?"

"Twenty-seven years."

The king stared.

"Twenty-seven years! I should have known it, had you been in the service a week. How old are you?"

"*Three weeks.*"

"Three weeks! and been in the service twenty-seven years."

The king turned purple with rage.

"Do you think I am a fool, or are you one yourself?" he shouted.

"Both."

"Seize that fellow!" said the king, looking as though he was going to burst. "Off with him to the guard-house!"

THE IRISH GIANT.

Pat remonstrated in Irish, which was not understood. Honour and glory and even money all looked cheap enough to him now, and he wished himself back on good old English soil.

The officer of the guard happened to know Pat's German acquirements, and he at once rightly guessed the situation, when the poor recruit was marched to the guard-house. He explained the whole matter to the king, who, for once, had a laugh that relaxed his usually clouded face.

The recruit was at once set at liberty.

"Faix," said Pat O'Flannigan, "niver pretind to know what ye don't know: else it is a whoppin' big blunder ye 'll be after gettin' into."

ERNEST WYNN'S STORY.

THE JOLLY OLD ABBOT OF CANTERBURY.

The minstrels used to sing of "Good King John," but the poets seem to be the only people who have had anything to say of King John's goodness. His forgiveness of the crafty old Abbot of Canterbury is the only good thing we ever heard of him, and we are a little suspicious that this incident may be too good to be true.

The Abbot of Canterbury was a thrifty old prelate, a lover of good cheer, and he lived right sumptuously, as the old prelates were wont to live during the reign of the Plantagenet kings. King John heard of the abbot's easy estate, and it made him very uneasy; for, being a sadly jealous man, he was always unhappy when he thought that another was better off than himself.

One day, there came to King John certain busy people, who said, —

"Do you know how many servants the Abbot of Canterbury keeps in his house?"

"No."

"An hundred."

"That is more than I keep in a palace!"

"Do you know how many gold chains the abbot has to hang over his coats of velvet?"

"No."

"Fifty."

"That is more than can be found among the jewels of the Crown! I will visit the Abbot of Canterbury. He has lived so long in luxury that he has lived long enough."

Then King John put on a terrible face, which must have been terrible indeed, for at the best he wore no merciful countenance, and he rode over to the grand old abbey, and summoned before him the luxury-loving abbot.

"How now, father abbot?" said the king sternly. "I hear that thou keepest a better house than I. That, sir, is treason, — high treason against the crown."

"My liege," said the abbot, "I never spend anything but what is my own. I trust that your Grace would do me no hurt for using for the comfort of others what I myself have earned."

"Yes, father abbot, thy offence is great. The safety of the kingdom demands thy death, and thou shalt die. Still, as thy learning is great, and as thou art esteemed a man of wit, I will give thee one chance of saving thy life."

" Name it, my liege."

" When I come again to this place, and stand among my liegemen with my crown on my head, thou shalt answer me three questions."

" Name them, my liege."

" Thou shalt tell me, first, how much I am worth, and that to a single penny.

" Thou shalt tell me, secondly, how long a time it would require for me to ride around the whole world.

" Thou shalt tell me, thirdly, what I am thinking."

" Oh, these are hard questions, — hard questions for my shallow wit," said the abbot, with a fallen face. " But if you will give me three weeks to consider them, I think I may answer your Grace."

" I give thee three weeks' space; that is the longest thou hast to live. If then thou canst not answer well these questions three, thy lands and thy livings shall become the Crown's."

The king departed, and the poor abbot sat down with a clouded brow and a heavy heart, and was at his wits' end.

At last, in utter despair of forming any answer himself, he ordered his horse, and rode over to Oxford and Cambridge to consult the doctors. Here he tarried many days, but

> " Never a doctor was there so wise,
> That could with his learning an answer devise."

With a heart more heavy, and a brow more dark, then

> " Home rode the abbot of comfort so cold."

As he was riding slowly, near the grounds of the old, old abbey, and marked the golden crosses gleaming above the great shadows of the trees, and reflected that he soon would cease to enjoy the pleasures of the place, his head dropped upon his breast, and the tears wet his cheek. As he dismounted, he saw a jolly shepherd — one of his own servants — going to the fold.

" How now, my lord abbot? " said the shepherd; " right welcome you are home! What news do you bring from the king? "

" Sad, sad news, shepherd! I have but three days more to live, if I do not answer him questions three."

" And what are the questions three? "

" First, to tell him, as he stands in yon place among his liegemen with the gold crown on his head, what he is worth, and that to a single penny.

"Secondly, to tell him how long it would take him to ride around the world.

"Thirdly, to tell him what he is thinking."

"Then cheer up, cheer up, my lord abbot! Did you never hear that a wise man may learn wit of a fool? They say I much resemble you. Lend me your gown and a horse and a serving-man, and I will stand in your place and will answer the king's questions."

The abbot brightened a little at this, and answered, —

"Horses and serving-men thou shalt have, and sumptuous apparel, with crozier and mitre, and rochet and cope, fit to appear before the Roman Pontiff himself."

The appointed day came, and the king stood in the designated place with his golden crown on his head and a great retinue of nobles glittering around him. The supposed abbot soon made his appearance, and took his position in the presence of the court.

"Now welcome, sir abbot!" said the king. "Thou dost faithfully keep the appointed day. Now answer correctly my questions three, and thou shalt save both thy life and thy livings."

"Well, my liege, but to answer correctly I must speak the truth."

"And that thou shalt. Now tell me what I am worth, and that within a single penny!"

"Twenty-nine pence. Judas betrayed his Lord for thirty, and since thou art willing to betray the Church, I think that thou must be one penny the worse than he."

The king received the answer with unexpected good-humour. He laughed heartily and exclaimed, —

"Why, why, my father abbot, I did not think that I was worth so little!

"And now, jolly priest," he continued, "tell me just how long it would take me to ride around the world."

"You must rise with the sun, and ride with the same until it riseth on the next morning, when you will have ridden the circuit of the world in just twenty-four hours."

The king laughed again, and said, —

"I did not think I could do it so soon. But now comes the question that will put your wits to the test. What do I think?"

"You think I am the Abbot of Canterbury, but I am not. I am a poor shepherd, and that you may see [throwing off his cloak]; and I have come to beg pardon for the abbot and for myself."

Then the king laughed more heartily than ever, and he sent the jolly shepherd back to his master with a full and free pardon.

"Four nobles a week
Will I give to thee
For this merry jest
Thou hast shown unto me.
And tell the old abbot,
When thou com'st home,
Thou hast brought him a pardon
From good King John."

MASTER LEWIS'S STORY.

THE LITTLE OLD MAN IN THE FOREST.

The Christmas story I am about to tell is well known to German children, all of whom go tripping through fairyland in the golden days of childhood. It was written by a good German baron, Frederic de la Motte Fouqué, who wrote the beautiful fairy story "Undine," about which all our readers have heard. It does not appear, however, in the popular translations of the works of the delightful old baron. It is quite a romance in the original, but I have reduced it to a very brief and simple story.

The nobleman who wrote it, and who loves good people and children almost as much as Hans Christian Andersen loved them, declares that this is a story that ought to be told. He does not say why; he leaves his readers, young and old, to guess that by their own firesides. So, you see, the story is something of a riddle,—one must live in a particular way to find it out.

Berthold was a German merchant. He travelled much from city to city. In Germany there are long, dark forests, through which he often journeyed.

The defiles in these forests, and especially those in the Hartz Mountains, are very narrow and perilous. The rocks are weird, and to the superstitious seem ghostly.

At some points the shadows of men and animals are magnified at sunset and sunrise by the atmosphere, and they appear like great figures in the air; and this and other natural phenomena have given rise to fearful stories of spectres, which the simple-hearted foresters believe.

One evening, Berthold became bewildered in one of these forests. He was riding on horseback; and, just as the far sunset was flaming over the tall tops of the trees above him, he was startled to find he had ridden out of his way. He carried great treasure in his saddle-bags,—jewels, ready money, and bills of exchange. In the recesses of the forests there were robbers.

As he was proceeding along a lone defile, after nightfall, he espied a man walking in the foot-path before him. He called to him, saying, —
"Who are you?"

DEFILE IN THE HARTZ MOUNTAINS.

"I am a collier. I live with my family apart from the world, in this forest."
"Can you give a stranger who has lost his way a night's lodging?"

"I have no right to refuse hospitality to a stranger. In God's name, you are welcome."

Berthold followed the man till they came to a little cottage. The good wife met them at the door with a lamp, and a happy family of children greeted the collier's return.

The evening passed pleasantly. The merchant told stories of his journeys, and soon felt at home among the children gathered lovingly around him.

At last it was proposed that they should sing. The sweet voices of the children were just joining in a merry roundelay, when a sudden and loud knocking was heard at the door. The children stopped singing, and the collier said firmly: "In the name of God, come in!"

Upon this, the door slowly opened, and a little old man, of gentle appearance and manners, came stealing in, greeting the family courteously, and taking the lowest place at the table. His garments were of some ancient pattern; he seemed wan and woe-begone, as though reduced by disease. Berthold gazed at him with a feeling of great curiosity and surprise, but said nothing. He once met the little old man's eye: there was something in it so deeply mysterious that he felt a chill creeping over him, and he began to be restless and ill at ease.

At last the little old man folded his hands, and, turning to the collier, said, — "It is the hour of prayer."

The collier at once began to sing "Now all the woods are sleeping," in which the whole family joined, filling the house with such delightful music that the merchant listened like one enchanted.

Presently a voice rose above the rest. It startled Berthold, and made the cottage tremble. It was the little old man's.

The family knelt down, and the collier prayed. Then they all rose up with loving words, and the little old man glided out of the door, bowing as humbly as when he came in.

But presently the door opened again, and the little old man once more appeared. He threw a look of fearful wildness upon Berthold, then disappeared, the door closing after him with violence.

"He is a little touched in mind," said the merchant, nervously.

"He is perfectly harmless," said the collier. "I have not seen any evil in him for a long time. But," he added, "the only chamber I can give you for the night has a door that does not shut very tightly; *he* comes into it in the night, but do not fear him; if you do not think any evil thought or do any evil act, he will go out of his own accord."

Berthold's heart was now far from tranquil. He pressed his portmanteau of treasures close to his side as the collier lighted him up the narrow stairway to his room.

IN THE HARTZ MOUNTAINS.

He lay down, placing his portmanteau and weapons beside him on the bed; but he could not sleep. He remembered what the collier had said about the little old man, that the safeguard against him was the absence of all evil thoughts and acts. In this respect the collier's family seemed secure; but the merchant knew how great was his own greed for gain; how it made him hard and uncharitable, and he tried to put away all evil thoughts and to think of the hymn, "Now all the woods are sleeping," lest the little old man should appear.

A little past midnight he fell into a troubled sleep, and his mind began to wander over his schemes for gain. He was dreaming of the good bargain he had made, or expected to make, when he was startled by a noise close by. He raised himself in bed, and saw the little old man in the moonlight, moving about the room. The merchant at first looked upon him with a feeling of curiosity rather than alarm or anger, and while he did so, all was well. But he at last became irritable under the disturbance, and when the little old man at last approached the bed, Berthold's irritability kindled into anger, and wicked thoughts began to fill his mind, and he found it hard to restrain his lips from evil words.

At last, the little old man touched the portmanteau containing the merchant's treasures. This was too much. The merchant's caution forsook him, and he was filled with rage.

"Back! you vile robber! back, from my baggage!" he exclaimed, seizing his pistols. The little old man started back, as in terror. He seemed to be in an agony of prayer. A change came over his face. He appeared conscious of it, and, going toward the door, disappeared.

Berthold gazed after him, and then remembered the collier's admonition in regard to the danger of evil thoughts. He wished that he had acted differently, for he would bring no evil on the family.

There was a sound at the latch; the door opened, when an evil-looking giant, wearing a red mantle, appeared. He laughed wildly, and said: "I begin to be free again. You have made me *grow!*"

Berthold saw that the giant was none other than the little old man.

The merchant leaped from his bed and discharged his pistol. The giant vanished, growing taller and more fearful as he disappeared.

In a moment, the collier hurried up the stairs.

"In the name of God," said he, rushing into the room, "what have you been doing to our house-spirit?"

"House-spirit!" said Berthold, like one in a dream. "What do you mean?"

"He has just gone out of the house," said the collier, "perfectly monstrous in his size, and inflamed with fury!"

But the collier saw that the merchant did not understand him, and he entreated him to go down into the common apartment where all of the family, aroused by the report of the pistol, had now met. The children shrunk away from him as he entered the room, and the collier's wife was in tears.

"And now," said the good woman, "we must live all those years over again."

"This may all seem strange to you," said the collier to the merchant; "but when my wife and I first came to the cottage to live, we found it haunted by a terrible spectre, such as I have just seen disappear. But I said to myself, I will not fear him, for if I am a truly Christian man no power of evil can harm me. I will overcome him with a good life, and he shall not overcome me. So, in the name of God, I remained. Red Mantle — for such is his name — appeared to us continually, but we ceased to fear him. I brought up my little ones to believe that nothing could harm them while they trusted in God; and that any spectre would grow less and less who dwelt in a family which had loving hearts and lived pure lives. So Red Mantle at last became my little ones' playmate. We restrained our dispositions, we guarded our thoughts, we loved each other, we prayed together much; and the spectre began to grow more gentle and to shrink in size, year by year, until he became the dwarf you saw when he came in the evening to prayers. All evil disappeared from his face, and we all loved him as a meek and harmless house-spirit, and expected that he would soon be released from this troubled state and vanish forever."

The next morning, the merchant left the cottage. Years passed away; he travelled from city to city, and into countries remote from Germany, but he never forgot the experiences of that night.

One afternoon, near sunset, he found himself on the borders of the same forest as before, and he resolved again to strike down the defile and see what had become of the good collier family.

It was somewhat late when the cottage appeared before him. He dismounted and entered. They were singing, "Now all the woods are sleeping." It was the hour of prayer!

The merchant knelt down beside the white-haired old man, expecting every moment the house-spirit would reappear. But the little old man did not come. Only a soft light was shed abroad amid the shadows of the room, and a sweet, low melody arose, like the touch of the most delicate fingers on finely attuned musical-glasses.

It was all that remained of the house-spirit, for the collier and his family had all these years lived pure and holy lives.

"That was once our house-spirit," said the collier; "but it can only now make its presence known to us as a gentle light and as a strain of music, sweet and low. We have subdued him by innocence and prayer."

SUPPOSED SPECTRES.

Wyllys Wynn's contribution to the entertainment was next on the programme, and he presented a quaint ballad, singing it and playing the accompaniment on the piano with much expression. We think the carol must have been very old.

"I saw three ships come sailing in,
 On Christmas in the morning;
Three goodly ships came sailing in,
 On Christmas in the morning;
And what was in those ships all three?
 On Christmas in the morning,
The Holy Babe and Sweet Mary,
 On Christmas in the morning.

"I saw three ships come sailing in,
 On Christmas in the morning;
Three goodly ships came sailing in,
 On Christmas in the morning.
But whither sailed those ships all three?
 On Christmas in the morning,
They sailed straight into Bethlehem,
 On Christmas in the morning.

"Now all the bells on earth did ring,
 On Christmas in the morning;
For in the heavens the angels sing,
 On Christmas in the morning;
And all the souls on earth shall sing,
 On Christmas in the morning;
And all of us rejoice amain
 On Christmas in the morning."

George Howe related the story of Edward IV., and the Tanner of Tamworth. The tanner not knowing the king, whom he met hunting, purchased the king's horse, and putting a cowhide on the back of the spirited animal attempted to ride him. The animal had only been trained to carry gentlemen on fine saddles; he was a steed of great pride and fine mettle; if a common rough soldier were to attempt to ride him, he would run like a deer and toss him like a ball. The horse resented the cowhide, and ran away with the tanner, who returned to the king indignant, and accused him of cheating him in the trade.

When the tanner found he had been trading with the king, he was even more frightened than when trying to ride the royal horse.

One of the scholars, Charlie Leland, gave an account of the early history of Alfred the Great, and described with much tact the scene in the cowherd's house on the Island of the Nobles (Athelney), when the cowherd's wife, thinking the king to be a mere shiftless wanderer, left him one day to watch the cakes that were baking by the fire. The king, dreaming of his misfortunes, let the cakes burn. When the woman returned, she sprang to the fire and turned the already blackened cakes, exclaiming, —

"You are too proud to turn the loaves, but I have no doubt you will be glad enough to eat them."

Wyllys Wynn next read an original poem, which ended the story-telling for the evening.

PROCOPIUS AND THE CHILDREN.

I will tell you a tale that the minstrels sung,
On the banks of the Saale, calm and fair,
When summer fruited the hills, and hung
Her golden moon in the golden air,
  Over the town of Naumburg.

Procopius was a Teuton bold,
He rode a white horse, bedecked with gold;
He rode a white horse, with captains ten,
At the head of an hundred thousand men,
  Far, far from the town of Naumburg.

And he and his goodly captains ten,
And his hundred thousand valorous men,
In the summer time came marching down
To the gates of the grand old German town,
  The beautiful town of Naumburg.

He planted his camp where the roses bloomed,
His pavilion rose in a vale perfumed,
Where the murmurous air was full of bees,
And reddened the boughs of the cherry-trees,
  Near the beautiful town of Naumburg.

ALFRED THE GREAT WATCHING THE PEASANT'S LOAVES.

THE ZIGZAG CLUB'S CHRISTMAS STORIES.

The stores of the city were nearly gone,
The wine was spent, and low was the corn, —
"All hope is lost," the people said :
"Strong walls are weak that have no bread.
　　Alas ! for the town of Naumburg."

A pedagogue came to the Saxon lords,
And spake to them these wonderful words :
"There are many ways of conquering,
And he who takes the heart of the king
　　May win for the town of Naumburg.

"Procop is clever, Procop is fat,
He children loves, now mark ye that ;
The children have power his heart to take,
And he may spare, for the children's sake,
　　The beautiful town of Naumburg.

"To-night, when he summons his council of state,
I will send the little ones out of the gate ;
And they shall kneel before him, and say, —
'Oh, good Procopius ! spare, we pray,
　　The beautiful town of Naumburg !'

"And they shall take the tender place
In Procopius' heart, and win his grace ;
And he will be well pleased to spare,
For the sake of the innocent children's prayer,
　　The beautiful town of Naumburg."

The lords were glad. At the sunset hour
The great bell rung in the signal tower ;
The warder lifted the iron gate,
And under it passed, with hope elate,
　　The boys and girls of Naumburg.

Procop came out of his tasselled tent,
And toward the city he gazed and went.
And met the children upon the way —
"Ho ! ho ! my little ones, whither to-day,
　　From the beautiful town of Naumburg ?"

"Oh, good Procop, have pity, have pity !
The corn and wine are low in the city ;
Oh, pity us, pity us, or we die !"
And the children all began to cry,
　　Near the foodless town of Naumburg.

Now great Procopius tried to be bad,
But so good and tender a heart he had
That he tried in vain. He heaved a sigh,
And a tear stood in his mild blue eye,
    For the beautiful town of Naumburg.

He put his hand on the little ones' hair,
And kissed their cheeks, so young and fair,
And his heart was won its tender place,
And he bent on the children a smiling face,
    Near the beautiful town of Naumburg.

He saw the broad sun hanging low,
And bade the soldiers quickly go,
And bring some fruit from the cherry-trees;
Then he took the children upon his knees,
    Near the beautiful town of Naumburg.

The cherries were brought — they were large and sweet —
Procopius bid the children eat.
The children feasted merrily then,
And waited upon them the captains ten,
    Near the beautiful town of Naumburg.

"Prepare to march!" said Procopius then,
To the master of horse, and the captains ten, —
"The city is famished and full of woe,
And the children must not starve, you know,
    In the beautiful town of Naumburg."

The summer moon, with a softened light,
Hung over the banks of the Saale that night;
But the master of horse, and the captains ten,
Had led the hundred thousand men
    Far, far from the town of Naumburg.

Procopius' memory long was dear;
The people honored it every year.
You have heard of the Cherry Feast, I know,
How the children of Saxony used to go
    To the beautiful town of Naumburg.

CHAPTER III.

A NEW JOURNEY PROPOSED.

PLANS FOR A NEW MIDSUMMER JOURNEY. — MASTER LEWIS'S ILL HEALTH. — HE PROPOSES TO GO TO THE AZORES. — PORTUGAL AND SPAIN. — TOMMY TOBY AND WYLLYS WYNN OBTAIN PERMISSION TO ACCOMPANY HIM. — HIS FAREWELL ADDRESS TO THE CLUB. — SEVERAL OF THE BOYS WISH TO MAKE A JOURNEY TO CLASSIC LANDS. — AN AMBITIOUS PLAN. — GREECE. — MOUNT PARNASSUS.

BOYS who have travelled once are eager to travel again, and about the middle of the winter term several of the boys of the academy, whose parents had liberal means, began to make plans for a midsummer tour in Europe.

"Since I have been reading Virgil," said Wyllys Wynn, "I have wished to go to the places visited by Æneas in his wanderings. I think a Zigzag journey to the places celebrated in the Iliad, Odyssey, and the Æneid would be the most interesting that a school-party could make."

"I do not expect to be able to make a tour abroad," said George Howe; "my father could not afford the expense of it. But I think a journey to the ruins of the old Roman and Grecian empires would be fine, and midsummer excursions on the Mediterranean must be delightful. I only wish I could make such a journey; it would be education for a lifetime."

"Perhaps you will win the prize for the best scholarship," said Tommy Toby. "You are leading your classes now. Should you get the hundred dollars offered, it would go far towards meeting the expense."

"Not far for such a journey as that," said George.

"But you know just how to plan and economize; and you, if you would put your wits to work as you did when we went abroad last year, might make one hundred dollars go a good way."

"But I have not secured the prize yet," said George.

This conversation led to the discussion of a summer tour abroad in the Club. Several of the boys were sure that their parents would allow them to make such a trip, if Master Lewis would consent to accompany them. It was agreed to ask him to plan an excursion to Latin lands, or to the lands whose history formed the subject of their classical studies, — those chiefly on the shores of the Mediterranean.

While the subject was under discussion, a misfortune befell the academy: Master Lewis became ill. For weeks he did not visit the schoolroom, his assistants doing his customary work.

It was at last announced in the school that he was recovering.

One March day he came into the schoolroom, with a thin face and a slow step. Every boy's face lighted up as he came through the door. A class was reciting. At the close of the recitation, he addressed the school.

"I have been very ill," he said, "and the doctors advise me to relinquish teaching for the present. You know how much I love my profession and my school. I shall hope to be at my desk again in the autumn. A sea voyage is the best medicine that I can now take. It has before relieved me of the trouble from which I am suffering. I expect to sail in a few weeks for Fayal. Should my health be improved, I shall visit Portugal, and make a spring journey through Spain to Barcelona; whence I shall sail to Marseilles, and at that city or at Nice shall probably spend a part of the summer. I only wish I might have as agreeable companions as I had on my last journey. My assistants in my absence will, perhaps more ably than I could do myself, conduct the school.

THE SHORES OF THE MEDITERRANEAN.

A NEW JOURNEY PROPOSED.

"I may not appear in the schoolroom again. I should be pleased, however, to accept an invitation to say a few words to the Club before I go."

He turned away from the familiar schoolroom evidently with a pang of pain. To teach was his life. This was the secret of his success.

"I wish to say something to you," said Wyllys Wynn to Tommy Toby, as soon as the day's session of the school was over. "I have a plan."

"And so have I."

"I wish to make that journey with Master Lewis."

"And so do I."

"My preparation for college is so nearly complete, that I could finish it on the voyage."

"I could mine."

"We could study together."

"Yes."

"My father, I am certain, would be willing I should go."

"My father would be glad to have me go," said Tommy, drolly.

"Let us each send a note to Master Lewis, asking him if he would be willing that we should accompany him."

"I will write mine to-day."

"And I mine."

The notes were written.

They received an immediate answer.

One was: —

MY DEAR WYLLYS, — I have been dreading this journey because I feared I should be very lonesome. I should not only be willing for you to accompany me, but I should regard it as a favor. I would, were I able, help you to complete your preparation for college during the journey, as a partial return.

Your attached teacher,

HERMAN LEWIS.

Tommy received a similar note.

Two days after he received this answer, Wyllys Wynn said to Tommy: —

"I have something to tell you."

"And I you."

"My father gives his permission."

"So does mine."

"Let me tell you a secret. Master Lewis is poor; my father knows his circumstances, and he promises to send him a cheque of $500 to help meet the expenses of his tour."

"My father writes that he shall liberally pay Master Lewis, if I go, for any instruction he may be able to give me during the journey."

"I showed my father's letter to Master Lewis."

"What did he say?"

"He said, 'Did ever a man have such kind friends?' and then he grew pale, and shed tears."

The arrangement of the two boys to go abroad with their teacher led the Club to a discussion of plans for Zigzag journeys during the midsummer vacation. Several of the new scholars wished to join Master Lewis at Marseilles, and make a European journey with him. These decided that they would choose the shores of the Mediterranean for a route.

"My health is too uncertain," said Master Lewis, "for me to give you positive encouragement now. Should I improve on my arrival at Lisbon, I would be willing to make an arrangement to have a party of pupils meet me at Paris or Marseilles, and to make with them an excursion along the shores of Italy, Sicily, and Greece; visiting the famous places in classic history. Such a journey would be a help in the study of the classics, and would be in itself delightful, provided that in the hot season much of the time was spent at healthy places on the seacoast."

Of course the Club made an arrangement for a meeting to receive the parting address from Master Lewis. The meeting was awaited

RUINS OF THE PARTHENON.

with an almost impatient interest. It was decided to make him a present on the occasion; and, as he expected to spend the spring in Spain, the works of Washington Irving were appropriately selected for the expression of respect and affection.

The evening appointed for the meeting found every member of the Club early in his seat. Master Lewis was received with a greeting that was at once so polite and appreciative that it touched his heart, the whole Club rising.

MASTER LEWIS'S ADDRESS.

"I have taken from the first an interest in your Club," Master Lewis began, "and when I found it proving a means of useful reading, I gave it a warm support. A right choice of books is usually a right choice of character.

"It is not those who have the greatest privileges, but those who have the most eager thirst for knowledge, who become eminently useful. For this reason self-instruction often proves the most valuable part of education. Cobbett learned grammar by the camp fire, and Rittenhouse calculated eclipses on the plough beam. One sneered at the great anatomist, Dr. Hunter, because Latin had not formed a part of his early studies. The Doctor regretted the defect of his education, which he could not help; but replied: 'I could teach *him* on a dead body what he never knew in any language, dead or living.' He had made the best use of the opportunities given him.

"The Duke of Argyle once observed a poor boy, the son of a laborer, reading a Latin copy of the 'Principia.' Thinking that the book had been taken from his own library, the duke ordered a servant to look to the matter. The boy claimed the book as his own.

"'*Your own?*' said the duke, coming forward.

"'Do *you* understand geometry, Latin, and Newton?'

"'I know something of each.'

"'But how came you by a knowledge of such things?'

"'A servant taught me to read, ten years ago. Does one need to know more than the alphabet, to learn all that he wishes? I first learned to read. I was informed that there was a science called arithmetic. I purchased a book of arithmetic, and I learned the science. I was told that there was another science called geometry. I bought the necessary books, and I learned geometry. I found that there were good books in these two sciences in Latin. I bought a dictionary, and I learned Latin. I learned also that there were books on these sciences in French. I bought a dictionary, and I learned French. This, my lord, is what I have been able to do, and it seems to me that one may learn everything who knows the alphabet.'

"That boy became an eminent man, and a member of the Royal Society. His name was EDMUND STONE.

"If I were a boy and had means as some of you have, I would immediately begin to collect in my room a library of my own. I would own a Bible and Concordance; a Webster's or Worcester's Dictionary, a standard Cyclopædia, Josephus' Works, Plutarch's Lives, Homer, Shakspeare, Addison, Milton, Tennyson, Longfellow, and Whittier; and as many histories and biographies as I could secure. If I were limited in means, as some of you are, I would begin to make a *scrap* library by buying low-cost books from the second-hand bookstores, and arranging them in the best bindings I could myself make. I wish to make the suggestion that you consider this subject at some meeting of the Club.

"Two of the boys of the school propose going with me to Spain. Let me suggest to them the reading of such books as Irving's 'Conquest of Granada,' his 'Alhambra,' his 'Columbus.'"

"Will you kindly allow me to interrupt you?" said Tommy Toby, rising.

There was great surprise in the school.

"Allow me," said Tommy, "in behalf of the Club, to present to *you* the 'Conquest of Granada,' the 'Alhambra,' and all of Irving's works. I may not be acting wisely in making the present at this point of time; pardon me if it be inopportune. The gift expresses our love. It was intended as a surprise, and if I have both surprised the Club and you, I hope neither will regard me as rude."

The good teacher choked with emotion, and said: —

"I certainly am glad to pardon the interruption. I thank you with more sincere feeling than I am able to express."

He continued: —

"To the works of Irving, which you have so thoughtfully and gracefully presented me, I would add Durden's 'History of Spain,' Southey's 'Cid,' Lockhart's 'Ballads,' and 'Don Quixote.'

"Some of you hope to visit the shores of the Mediterranean. Let me mention some of the scenes one might see, and let them suggest to you topics for reading.

ITALIAN BEGGARS.

"You would pass over the supposed course of the Argonauts in search of the Golden Fleece; you might follow the track of Ulysses and Æneas, or the missionary journey of the Apostle Paul.

"You might visit the field or plain of Troy, the ruins of Priam's palace, and the mounds of Hector, Achilles, and Ajax.

"You might see Parnassus, on whose top the gods were fabled to dwell; Corinth, with its remains of departed glory; Athens, with its Acropolis; Salamis, and the rocky throne on which Xerxes watched the greatest battle in history; Ætna, the fabled furnace of Vulcan; the island of the Cyclops, and nearly all the Latin associations of the old Roman empire. And at Rome you would see splendid churches, palaces, and pictures; grand ruins of the crumbled

ITALIAN MOUNTEBANKS.

empire that once ruled the world, and beggars and mountebanks everywhere. You would walk among beggars and mountebanks, and ride among beggars and mountebanks, and find empty and dirty hands stretched out to you on every side. Classic Italy is full of beggars, and while one eye is feasted with splendor, the other is tortured with scenes of misery; the lame, the halt, and the blind crawl out of the way as one's carriage sweeps on to the grand cathedral or palace. An American learns to love the free homes of his republic, even there.

"Whether he be rich or poor, I love the boy who is gathering resources

THE ROMAN FORUM.

for life in self-instruction. Emulate the examples I have given. The school room has its heroes.

"We read that Italy was twice conquered by the valor of youth; that the Persian went down before the genius of a boy; that Lepanto was won by a fiery-minded warrior, whose manhood had scarcely begun; that Gaston de Foix earned his bay leaves at Ravenna, at the age of twenty-two; and that Cortes conquered his way to the glittering domes of the Aztecs while the glow of youth was yet warm on his cheek. But there is something in the *moral* heroism which struggles through the allurements of youth to pre-eminence in knowledge, that is more noble than martial prowess. He who has made the most of his own abilities and has sublimated his own nature, is more heroic than he who has made desolations in the earth.

BEGGARS IN ROME.

"It is recorded of one of the noblest kings who ever wrought righteousness upon a throne, — ' In every work that he began in the service of the house of God, and in the law, and in the commandments, to seek his God, he did it with all his heart, and prospered.'

"'He did it with all his heart, and prospered.' This is the universal history of human success.

"'Go on! go on! no moments wait Go on! go on! thou canst not tell
 To help the right.   Thy mission here;
Be strong in faith, and emulate Whate'er thou doest, labor well,
The virtues of the good and great Nor let a doubt within thee dwell,
 With all thy might.   Or coward fear.
 Go on!   Go on!'"

At the next meeting of the Club plans for a vacation tour in classic lands were discussed. Only a few of the boys would be able to make the journey in case Master Lewis should consent to conduct it; but all the Club were interested in mapping out a route over which they would like to go.

"If I could go," said George Howe, "I should want the party to do something that other American boys have never attempted, — visit Delphi, climb up Mount Parnassus, the very spot where Apollo was believed to have had his seat."

"I have a new idea," said Tommy Toby. "A club should have a password, a legend. I propose that our password be *Parnassus*, and after we have been to Greece and climbed the mountain of Apollo and the Muses, that that be the legend of the Club."

The next day Tommy met Master Lewis, and said, —

"Is it possible for a party of travellers to ascend Mount Parnassus?"

"I think so. It is only about eight thousand feet to the summit, and villages and convents occupy sites on its sides. Delphi is on its southern side."

"Shall *we* be able to climb Parnassus?"

"I have not fully decided to make the journey to Greece. If I should recover my health, I should be unwilling to undertake it in company with any of my pupils unless it could be accomplished before the middle of July. The heat on the Mediterranean becomes very intense about this time, and the unhealthy season begins in August.

"The fathers of one or two of the boys have written to me about making such a journey. I have replied favorably, but I cannot fully decide until I reach Lisbon."

The Club began reading books on Grecian and Roman antiquities. Wordsworth's "Greece" became a favorite on account of its great number of illustrations. Several of the boys read parts of the translation of the Iliad and Odyssey; others took up Plutarch's Lives, and the Latin class pursued the study of Virgil with great interest and success.

A picture of Mount Parnassus and Delphi was hung up in the club room, which stimulated the reading of classical works and the desire to travel and to visit Greece.

VENICE.

CHAPTER IV.

FROM BOSTON TO LISBON.

AMUSEMENTS ON SHIPBOARD — AUNT VITEY'S QUEER STORY. — STORY OF DE SOTO. — STORY OF PONCE DE LEON. — THE AZORES. — VOLCANIC ISLANDS.

HOW little we thought," said Tommy Toby to Wyllys Wynn, as they met on the wharf, "that we should so soon make another voyage, when we landed here eight months ago!"

It was a mild March day, with interspaces of spring blue sky in the light gray clouds, when the iron steamship, "The Father of Waters," moved out of Boston Harbor, bound for the Azores and Madeira. Master Lewis and the boys, who for convenience we will still call THE CLASS, stood on deck and saw the city of Boston gradually disappear behind the forts and islands, and the gilded dome of the State House seemingly become lower and lower, and sink into the sea. Night came on with a brisk breeze, rainy and chill. The next morning found them rocking on the broad ocean.

The boys did not appear at the table at breakfast in the morning. Master Lewis rapped on the door of their state-room, which, after an ominous delay, was opened by Wyllys.

"How are you feeling this morning?" asked Master Lewis.

Tommy gave one glance at Master Lewis from his berth.

"*Dreadful!*" said Tommy. "That's how I feel. I feel just as I did on the former voyage, when I resolved that I would never, never again go to sea."

"What, never?" said Master Lewis, cheerfully.

"' Hard — '"

But Tommy was not able to make the expected quotation, and dropped his head on his pillow with a very white face.

The next day found the Class on deck. Time passed heavily. There was little to amuse the boys, and they found it hard, owing to the novelty of the situation, to discipline their minds to study. They however soon came to accustom themselves to their new circumstances; but after study their diversion consisted chiefly in looking at the various expressions of the sky and sea.

Master Lewis played with them a game which is a favorite on passenger steamers, called nine-billiards. It is simply a variation of the play-ground game of hop-scotch, rendered a little more difficult by a diagram and the rocking of the ship. A number of squares were chalked on the floor of the deck. These were numbered in the middle 5, 7, 9, etc. Wooden disks were tossed towards the diagram from a certain distance. If the disk rested outside of the diagram or on one of the lines, it counted for nothing, but if it rested in the division numbered 7 or 5 it counted for that number. The player who first made 100 won the game. The game could as well and better be played on land: it was made very humorous by the motion of the ship, which often caused the disk to fall very wide of the mark.

The boys had been reading intelligently concerning the ocean path over which they were going, — about the studies and dreams of Columbus in Lisbon, his voyages to the Azores, and that persevering voyage that bore him triumphantly westward, when he strained his eyes at latest twilight and earliest dawn to see fulfilled the visions that his charts and studies had so often revealed to him in Spain, Portugal, and Italy. They read aloud on deck the story of his arrest and imprisonment,

COLUMBUS LOOKING FOR LAND.

when he longed and prayed in his dungeon for freedom again to bear to the West the banner of the Cross and Castile, and dreamed that good spirits would help him to break the cruel chain. They read also Irving's account of the companions of Columbus, and were especially interested in the tragic story of Vasco Numez, the discoverer of the Southern Ocean, and of Juan Ponce de Leon, who discovered Florida, and sought to find there the fabled " Fountain of Youth." After reading the history of the last adventurer, Wyllys Wynn wrote a poem which he read to Master Lewis, and afterwards to a company of tourists, one evening, in the saloon.

The occasion on which Wyllys read the poem to the passengers somewhat resembled one of the meetings of the Zigzag Club. Several of the passengers related stories of the old Portuguese and Spanish voyagers and discoverers. Master Lewis's story related to De Soto, the discoverer of the Mississippi, and we give it here.

THE INDIAN'S PROPHECY.

That was an impressive scene that occurred on the banks of the Red River three hundred and fifty years ago. The old Spanish chroniclers, Garcillasso de la Vega among them, tell the tale of Fernando de Soto's wanderings, death, and burial as no American history I have ever read can do. They picture that thrilling scene to which I refer. Perhaps these old historians exaggerated, but they wrote in an age when men's minds were full of wonder at the discovery of a strange, new continent and its stranger inhabitants. They were fed on marvels, and it was, besides, a credulous and an ignorant age.

In all Spain there was no braver or wealthier knight than Fernando de Soto. He had fought with Pizarro in the conquest of Peru, and brought immense treasures from that country. He was of high birth, and so great a favorite with the King of Spain, Charles I., that that monarch conferred upon him the governorship of the lately discovered Island of Cuba, and made him viceroy over all the countries he might discover and subjugate.

He was already too wealthy to care much for treasure, but he was ambitious for power; and the discovery of the gold and silver mines which were said to exist in the Floridas he thought would raise him higher in the king's favor. But a greater inducement than even all this to the brilliant knight was the "Fountain of Youth" which was said to exist in this new, strange world.

This "Fountain of Youth" was an old fable of ancient peoples, and it was revived in the fourteenth and fifteenth centuries and became a fixed belief, particularly among the Spaniards. A decrepit old person going down into the waters of this magical fountain would emerge in the first flush of youth.

Now De Soto was no longer a young man, though still in the prime of life, about forty; and he craved above all things in the world a prolonged youth to enjoy the gifts of fortune which had been lavished upon him. He never doubted that he should find the fountain; in fact, he was a person who had not learned the meaning of the word "failure." *That* was to be his latest lesson.

In 1539 he landed on the shores of the bay "Espiritu Santo," with twelve hundred men, three hundred of the number having been raised at his own expense. He sent his vessels back to Havana, thus virtually closing all retreat to his men.

We cannot follow him in his painful wanderings. Harassed on every side by the Indians, encumbered by heavy armor, the weight of which sank the horses in the swamps and morasses they had to traverse, fainting under the hot Southern sun, the adventurers made their way through Georgia, the Cherokee country, Tennessee, and Kentucky.

No wealth was there for them, no "Fountain of Youth." Nothing but a wily and savage foe, who harassed their every step, though the Spaniards were usually victorious in the skirmishes. They returned southward through the valley of the Tombigbee to Mobile Bay, and there they encountered the Mobilians, a tribe of the Natchez Indians, who fought more like evil spirits than men.

The horrors of that siege of Mobile even the Spanish chroniclers shudder to relate. Eleven thousand Indian warriors fell in defence of their capital. A thousand women threw their children into the flames of their burning homes and plunged after them.

Tradition tells a thrilling story of the siege. One of the women, as she threw her children into the fire and prepared to leap after them, paused one moment to call a curse on her enemies.

She lifted her hand towards heaven and prayed.

"Let them be destroyed," she said, "by land and water! Let the forests be strewn with the slain! May the soil they have ravaged and reddened with innocent blood reject even the bones of their cruel leader! The Great Spirit will avenge us! The woes of Heaven will follow the invader!"

De Soto tried to laugh off the impression left by this prophecy, but his tide

COLUMBUS IN PRISON.

of misfortune set in with the destruction of Mobile, or Manvilla, as it was called. In one night the Chickasas killed forty of his men and fifty horses with burning arrows. Neither the men nor horses could be replaced in that hostile country.

Then commenced the most disastrous wanderings that the pen of the early historian has traced. The borders of the White River and the Arkansas were literally tracked by the dead Spaniards. Excessive fatigue, want of food, and the deadly swamp-fevers slew the strangers faster than the arrows of their savage foe. The woe of the Indian mother must have rung in their ears.

At last they entered the Red River. "It is a 'river of blood!'" exclaimed De Soto. "What a color! What desolate banks!

"Look at those gray festoons of moss, hanging like shrouds from the trees to the very water. Nothing is here but death and decay."

They stopped at its mouth, and then the illness against which De Soto had fought for some time mastered him. The fever-demon of the swamp had clutched the gallant knight.

Can you imagine a greater mockery of fate? Under the moss-draped trees, on the rotting leaves, a hasty pallet was spread; and on it the man of unbounded wealth, the flower of Spanish chivalry, whose fame was spread throughout Christendom, lay down to die.

He never doubted that his last hour had come, but he shuddered at the spot.

"Had it been anywhere else!" he muttered; "but those waves like blood, these funereal trees! It is too dreadful! Alvarado, are the Indians near the camp?"

"Very near," he answered. "They do not come out of ambush, but they harass us with their arrows at every turn."

He may now have recalled the Indian mother's prophecy. "Do not let them get my body, Alvarado. I do not care much for this worn-out shell, but, St. Iago! it is shocking to think of those savage infidels dishonoring the body of a Christian knight."

"I declare to you, on my faith as knight and gentleman, that the savages shall not touch your remains," Muscoso de Alvarado answered solemnly.

"Lift my head on your knee," gasped the dying knight. "Call my men, and let them hear my last commands."

They crowded around him. Only three hundred left of the twelve hundred gallant warriors who had landed, so full of hope and enterprise, on the continent of the New World.

"Friends," he said, "De Soto's race is run."

He held out his wasted hand.

"Swear on this hand, which never faltered in deadly stroke to foe or loving grasp to friend, that you will obey Muscoso de Alvarado as myself! I name him my successor, and he knows my wishes."

They swore, and then turning to the priest who stood beside his pallet, — "Father, I have done with time. Now shrive me from the sins which bar me from the peace of eternity."

But during the last ceremonies of the Catholic Church for the dying penitent De Soto's mind wandered. In his gasping whispers he told of the fabled Bimini, the "Fountain of Youth," which had brought him on the fatal quest. "A draught of water! quick, quick, for the love of Heaven!"

As the bitter, nauseous water of the red stream was put to his lips he drained the cup eagerly, gave a sigh of relief, and sank back. The black draught of death had stilled the restless fever of his ambitious life.

Where would they make De Soto's grave? The Spaniards dug it on the shore. They noticed that the Indians on the other side of the river were watching them. Their outposts, caught too, glimpses of dusky forms moving among the shadows of the swamp back of them.

The Spaniards knew that as soon as they moved from the spot the dead body of their leader would be dragged from its resting-place.

"This will not do," Alvarado said. "Close the grave, and after dark we will dig one in another spot."

That night they did not even dare take a torch to light their gloomy labors. In profound darkness they hollowed the grave, and silently laid De Soto's body within it.

Still further to disarm suspicion, the next morning they made a kind of tilting-ground above the grave, not only to harden the earth, but to deceive the watchful eyes which they knew were watching every movement.

The horses caracoled, the knights tilted, with their hearts full of anguish at this desecration of what, to them, was a hallowed spot.

They flattered themselves that the savages would not suspect the ruse. The Indians themselves hold the relics of their dead in such reverence that they would not be likely to think that this ghastly tournament was held over a grave.

But no precaution availed against the wily and numerous foe. Through a prisoner taken that day, or some friendly Indian spy the Spaniards had attached to their service, Alvarado heard that the exact spot of the grave was known to the enemy. With a heavy heart he summoned a hasty council, and then and there they decided upon a mode of sepulture which would prevent all possibility of desecration.

The body of the knight, clad in his heavy armor, was removed from the

BIVOUAC OF DE SOTO'S EXPEDITION IN FLORIDA.

grave. The trunk of a cypress tree was felled, hollowed out, and the corpse laid in one section of it. Taking boats, they rowed to the middle of the river, and lowered the strange coffin into the water. Heavily weighted as it was, it sank instantly under the slime and sand of the Red River.

Wyllys Wynn's poem was as follows: —

THE FOUNTAIN OF YOUTH:

A DREAM OF PONCE DE LEON.

A story of Poncé de Leon,
    A voyager, withered and old,
Who came to the sunny Antilles,
    In quest of a country of gold.
He was wafted past islands of spices
    As bright as the Emerald seas,
Where all the forests seem singing,
    So thick were the birds on the trees;
The sea was as clear as the azure,
    And so deep and so pure was the sky
That the jasper-walled city seemed shining
    Just out of the reach of the eye.
By day his light canvas he shifted,
    And rounded strange harbors and bars;
By night on the full tides he drifted,
    'Neath the low-hanging lamps of the stars.
Near the glimmering gates of the sunset,
    In the twilight empurpled and dim,
The sailors uplifted their voices,
    And sang to the Virgin a hymn.
" Thank the Lord!" said De Leon, the sailor,
    At the close of the rounded refrain;
"Thank the Lord, the Almighty, who blesses
    The ocean-swept banner of Spain!

" The shadowy world is behind us,
    The shining Cipango, before;
Each morning the sun rises brighter
    On ocean, and island, and shore.
And still shall our spirits grow lighter,
    As prospects more glowing unfold;
Then on, merry men! to Cipango,
    To the west, and the regions of gold!"

There came to De Leon, the sailor,
    Some Indian sages, who told
Of a region so bright that the waters
    Were sprinkled with islands of gold.
And they added : " The leafy Bimini,
    A fair land of grottoes and bowers,
Is there ; and a wonderful fountain
    Upsprings from its gardens of flowers.
That fountain gives life to the dying,
    And youth to the aged restores ;
They flourish in beauty eternal,
    Who set but their foot on its shores!"
Then answered De Leon, the sailor :
" I am withered, and wrinkled, and old ;
I would rather discover that fountain
    Than a country of diamonds and gold."

Away sailed De Leon the sailor;
    Away with a wonderful glee,
Till the birds were more rare in the azure,
    The dolphins more rare in the sea.
Away from the shady Bahamas,
    Over waters no sailor had seen,
Till again on his wondering vision
    Rose clustering islands of green.
Still onward he sped till the breezes
    Were laden with odors, and lo!
A country embedded with flowers,
    A country with rivers aglow,
More bright than the sunny Antilles,
    More fair than the shady Azores.
" Thank the Lord!" said De Leon, the sailor,
    As feasted his eye on the shores.
" We have come to a region, my brothers,
    More lovely than earth, of a truth ;
And here is the life-giving fountain, —
    The beautiful Fountain of Youth."

Then landed De Leon, the sailor,
    Unfurled his old banner, and sung ;
But he felt very wrinkled and withered,
    All around was so fresh and so young.
The palms, ever-verdant, were blooming,
    Their blossoms e'en margined the seas ;
O'er the streams of the forests bright flowers
    Hung deep from the branches of trees.

BURIAL OF DE SOTO.

"Praise the Lord!" sung De Leon, the sailor;
  His heart was with rapture aflame,
And he said: "Be the name of this region
  By Florida given to fame.
'Tis a fair, a delectable country,
  More lovely than earth, of a truth;
I soon shall partake of the fountain, —
  The beautiful Fountain of Youth!"

But wandered De Leon, the sailor,
  In search of that fountain in vain;
No waters were there to restore him
  To freshness and beauty again.
And his anchor he lifted, and murmured,
  As the tears gathered fast in his eye,
"I must leave this fair land of the flowers,
  Go back o'er the ocean, and die."
Then back by the dreary Tortugas,
  And back by the shady Azores,
He was borne on the storm-smitten waters
  To the calm of his own native shores.
And that he grew older and older
  His footsteps enfeebled gave proof,
Still he thirsted in dreams for the fountain, —
  The beautiful Fountain of Youth.

One day the old sailor lay dying
  On the shores of a tropical isle,
And his heart was enkindled with rapture,
  And his face lighted up with a smile.
He thought of the sunny Antilles,
  He thought of the shady Azores,
He thought of the dreamy Bahamas,
  He thought of fair Florida's shores.
And when his mind he passed over
  His wonderful travels of old,
He thought of the heavenly country,
  Of the city of jasper and gold.
"Thank the Lord!" said De Leon, the sailor,
  "Thank the Lord for the light of the truth,
I now am approaching the fountain, —
  The beautiful Fountain of Youth."

The cabin was silent: at twilight
  They heard the birds singing a psalm,
And the wind of the ocean low sighing
  Through groves of the orange and palm.

> The sailor still lay on his pallet,
> 'Neath the low-hanging vines of the roof;
> His soul had gone forth to discover
> The beautiful Fountain of Youth.

There was an old colored woman on board, called Aunt Vitey, who was going to Fayal in the service of a Southern family which had been spending the winter in Boston. She often amused herself by watching the boys play hop-scotch, especially when the sea was rough; and in this manner she easily made their acquaintance. She was a wonderful story-teller.

She seemed disposed to patronize one of the mulatto waiters, — a young man, who, by virtue of some education, carried to his menial offices an air of weary and superb indifference. But, in spite of his grand airs, he had a keen relish for Aunt Vitey's wonderful tales, and all his spare time was spent in listening to them.

One night the boys heard her and the waiter engaged in a hot altercation outside the cabin. Old Vitey's voice rose shrill.

"You say dem hairy dogs look like possums? Wot you see ob possums way off in Bosting, whar dere ain't no swamp fur 'em, nor holler tree, I reckon, whar dey kin live? Hush up, boy, and don't talk 'bout tings you don't know nothin' 'bout! You'se too 'ficious, caze you kin read and write a leetle; and you tink you've got all de larnin' in de world. But you can't tell *me* nothin' 'bout *possums;* ob all de contrayriest, knowinest creeters, dey takes de lead in de doxology ob Nater.

"If you'se kilt you'll stay kilt, I reckon." The boys' curiosity was excited by this vague, but suggestive declaration. They knew a story would follow, and they soon were at Aunt Vitey's side with ears pricked up in expectation. She seemed to feel flattered by their attention, and told a very odd story.

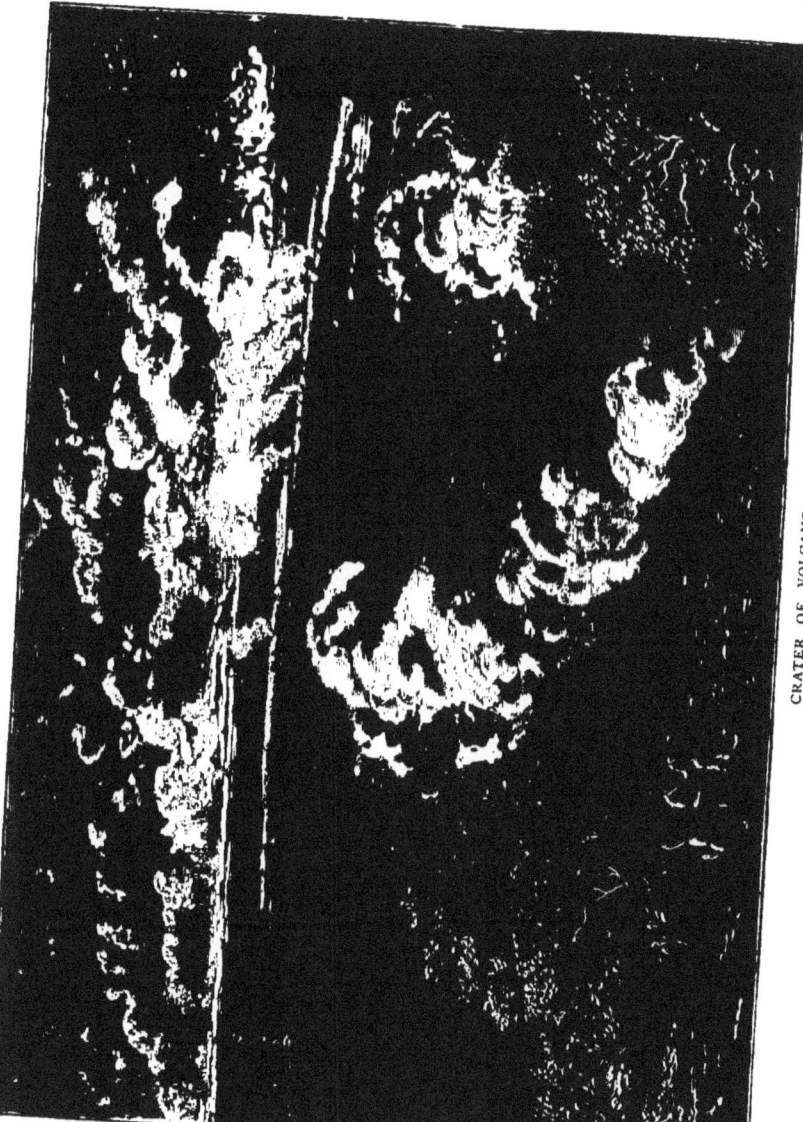

CRATER OF VOLCANO.

A SURPRISED COOK.

"Way down in Louisanny, whar I was brunged up, my ole massa's plantation had a big swamp back ob it, where possums and coons and 'gators was as plenty as skeeters. Jake, my old man, was a famous hunter; and wen his day's work was done, he ups wid his gun and goes a-huntin'. He was awful lazy, was Jake, 'cept 'bout huntin'; and den he was lively enough, caze he loved good eatin', possums 'specially. One day he brung a big fat possum, as dead and stiff as could be, and trows it down, and sez he, —

"'Ole 'ooman, I wants dat possum baked fur supper to-night, and don't grudge de stuffin'. I'll 'vite Sam Loomis to supper, for his wife she don't know how tō fix a possum like you.'

"'Well,' I sez, 'Jake, I'll make de stuffin' and I'll cook de possum; but you must clean and scra⁻e him.'

"'All rite,' Jake sez, a-stretchin' hisself 'fore de fire. 'But, Vitey, my feet's jest soakin' wet. Soon as dey dry a little, I'll come.'

"Den he ha, ha'd, and I tuck de possum and put it on de kitchen table, and sot to work on my stuffin'. I was gwine to show dat shifless 'ooman, Sam Loomis's wife, how a possum could be better'n any pig.

"De stuffin' was ready, but whar was Jake? De possum was, as I thought, growin' cold and stiff on de table, which ain't right; fur a possum to eat tender orter be dressed as soon as it's kilt. I went after Jake, and, bless you! de lazy nigger was layin' back on his chair a-snorin' away, and de bare soles ob his feet jest smokin' 'fore de fire. He nebber had no feelin' in his foots no how. I shuck him and I shuck him eber so long, 'fore he wake up and cum to his senses. Den he jumps up and sez, —

"'Gib me de carbin knife and lemme sharpen it.' And he got his razor strop and he stropped away for nearly half an hour; and den we goes to de kitchen, and Jake he marches up to de table.

"'Whar you done put de possum, Vitey?' he calls out.

"'Rite under yer nose,' I sez; but it wan't dar, and it wan't under de table, nor nowhar in de kitchen.

"What do you tink had happened? De varmint had cum to hisself, and got out de winder!

"Jake hollered, 'Look his tracks here on de floor and de winder, and de blood outside whar he jumped! He's cheated us, playin' he was dead and stiff, de deceitful ole ting!'

"We jest stood dar and looked at each oder. Jake was mad, and I was madder, 'caze it was his laziness which kep him from tendin' to de creeter in time. My mouf was fixed for possum, and it hurt me so bad I jest sot down and cried and scolded, till I scared Jake.

"'Don't take on so, ole 'ooman,' he sez; 'your nice stuffin' shan't go beggin'. I'll kill de rooster, — 't ain't no 'count in de yard, — and we'll hab a nice bake anyhow.'

"I ups and goes to de bowl ob stuffin' on de table. If you b'lieve me, de bowl was as empty as de palm ob my hand!

"I looked at Jake and he looked at me. I held up de bowl *so*.

"'Jake!' sez I, 'what yer s'pose dat audacious varmint has ben gone and done?'

"'Ole 'ooman!' Jake sez, 'he's gone and done jest what you was gwine to do.'

"'Wha' dat?' sez I.

"'He's put dat stuffin' jes whar ye's gwine to put it.'

"'An' whar has dat stuffin' gone?' sez I.

"'Ole 'ooman, ole 'ooman!' sez Jake, 'dar be many mysterious tings in dis here world. An' whar dat stuffin's be done gone, de possum only knows.'

"Would you ha' b'lieved it, dat audacious varmint had stuffed hisself wid my stuffin', and gone off to sleep in some holler tree or oder. Dat is what I calls animal intelligence."

Tommy and Vitey became fast friends. She entertained him usually several times a day with stories of "ole times of Louissany."

"I likes stories," she would say, "dat makes yo'r eyes stick out; and I alwas makes it a p'int to make yo'r eyes stick out 'fore I gits troo, I dun duz."

Tommy liked that kind of stories, too; and it must be confessed that even Master Lewis often sat down within hearing distance, when she told tales of the "ole cabin in de Souf."

After the first few days of the voyage the weather for March was unusually pleasant. Besides Aunt Vitey's stories, Tommy found many diversions on shipboard. There was a goat on board, which he obtained a ready permission to care for and to milk. The ship was like a great gymnasium to him, and he performed many feats of climbing, swinging, and balancing, both in the rigging and about the decks and cabins.

After sailing nine days the boys came upon deck one morning, and were surprised to see a dark object towering in the mist. The fog gradually passed away, and the sun came out, and the gray object seemed changing into a hill in the sea, terraced with gardens. It was the island of Flores. They had reached the Azores. The ship stopped at Fayal, Terceira, and St. Michael, three islands that were once flames and lava pouring forth from the sea. On the island of Pica, one of the Azores, there is a lava-covered peak 7613 feet high, — much higher than Mount Washington. What an immense conflagration in the sea there must have been when this island of fire was poured forth from the hidden furnaces of the earth! Each island has its caldeira, or extinct crater, black, awe-inspiring openings of these chimneys of the sea. The Class visited two of these.

MILKING A GOAT.

The air on these islands was soft and mild; the towns were quaint, and the people affable and light-hearted.

As the Class left the Azores they watched the peak of Pica glowing in the sun and apparently sinking in the sea.

"Is that the highest volcanic peak in the sea?" asked Tommy.
"No," said Master Lewis, "the volcanic island of Kliutschewsk is just *twice* as high."

"Have any volcanic islands arisen from the sea in recent times?"

"Yes; in 1776 a volcano of smoke poured out of the sea in the Pacific Ocean, near Unalaska; the crater of a volcano rose above the water, and a column of flame issued forth which illuminated the sea and the country around for many miles. In 1831 Grahame's Island arose in a volcanic mass in the Mediterranean; the waves afterwards washed it away. The interior of the earth is probably a mass of fire. A volcano is

SWINGING.

fire seeking vent. Lava from Vesuvius has been thrown at a height of 10,000 feet, indicating a propelling force that is incalculable. A stream of lava once flowed down the side of Hecla which was in itself equal to a mountain. It travelled fifty miles in forty-two days, destroying life as it went."

The ship next arrived at Madeira, that island of perpetual springtime, where the thermometer only varies as a rule from 64° to 74° during the year, and where nearly all the flowers of the tropics bloom, and most of the luscious fruits of the sunlands grow.

From Funchal, Madeira, the Class sailed on a Portuguese boat for Lisbon.

CHAPTER V.

FROM LISBON TO GRANADA.

LISBON. — STORY OF THE GREAT EARTHQUAKE. — COIMBRA. — THE MOORS. — STORY OF THE CID. — STORY OF INEZ DE CASTRO. — BADAJOS. — A ZIGZAG JOURNEY ON HORSEBACK. — SEVILLE. — MURILLO.

HE morning broke; the air grew warmer, and in the purple distance a rim of land, like a dream of Paradise, seemed lightly suspended between the blue sea and flushing sky. The air was wonderfully transparent, and there was a freshness in it that told the class that land was near.

The boat was approaching Portugal, the land of the old navigators; it was cleaving the waters over which Vasco de Gama sailed to discover the way to India around the perilous African Cape.

The mouth of the Tagus was soon reached, and palace-crowned heights were seen glimmering in the clear air. Then the city of Lisbon, light and airy as one of Turner's pictures, seemed to rise over the beautiful harbor.

The approach to the city from the sea is defended by the Castle Belem. This picturesque structure once stood on a rock in the Tagus, but a deposit of sand has connected it with the mainland. It is a fortress and a church. Its convent was founded in 1499, as a thank-offering to God for the safe return of Vasco de Gama and for the success of his expedition to India. The portal of the church that faces the sea is adorned with the statue of Dom Henrique, the pioneer in naval discovery.

TRAVELLING IN SPAIN.

Lisbon, a city about the size of Providence, R. I., is built partly on the shores of the Tagus and partly on the adjoining hills. Its suburbs extend some five miles along the river. The appearance of the city from the river is truly picturesque and magnificent.

THE TOWER OF BELEM.

The Class was landed at the Praça do Commercio, which is said to be the finest square in Europe. It is five hundred and sixty-five feet long, five hundred and twenty broad, and is surrounded on three sides with splendid edifices and great commercial palaces.

The most beautiful part of Lisbon occupies the site of the devastation and ruin of the great earthquake in 1755.

THE GREAT EARTHQUAKE

At Lisbon on Nov. 1, 1755, was the most awful calamity of the kind that ever occurred in the Old World.

It was a still and beautiful morning. The sun had risen, dissipating the fog that hung over the city and harbor, and promising a serene autumn day. Suddenly a subterranean thundering began, as though the foundations of the earth were giving way. Almost immediately the earth was upheaved as from some internal convulsion. The churches and houses were overturned like blocks of wood. The earth sank, crushing in an instant thirty thousand human beings. The dying lay everywhere under the weight of ruined walls, imploring aid which no human power could render. Sir Henry Falkland, who once lived near Boston in a grand colonial mansion, was in Lisbon at this time. He was travelling, and had in his service a beautiful servant-girl, named Agnes Surrige, who had quite won his affections as he had met her at an inn in Marblehead. She escaped being struck by the falling ruins in the overturn of the city. She found Sir Henry buried under a building, and rescued him by dragging him out of a strange position with her teeth. He afterwards married her, and she became Lady Agnes, and is celebrated in one of the poems of Dr. Holmes.

The earthquake lasted but two or three minutes. The churches were filled with worshippers at the time, and became the tombs of those who were crushed as they fell. Nearly all the houses came crashing down. In one family only four persons survived out of thirty-eight members.

The destruction around Lisbon was as great as in the city. The sea retired from the harbor, leaving the bar dry; then it came rushing back again in a wave sixty feet high, which carried everything to destruction before it. The seaport at Setubal, some twenty miles from Lisbon, totally disappeared. On the African side of the Mediterranean, in the vicinity of Morocco, the earth opened and swallowed up a town of eight thousand inhabitants. More than sixty thousand people in Lisbon and its vicinity perished.

The shock was felt in England and America. The ocean was terribly agitated, and ships were overturned and swallowed up. The mountains of Portugal were shaken to their bases; some of them were broken asunder, and many volcanic mountains in the south of Europe seemed to rekindle their fires.

The earthquake was caused by some subterranean change or convulsion of the earth's substance; but what can never be known.

DOORWAY OF SANTA MARIA, BELEM.

GATE OF THE CASTLE OF PINTRA DE CINTRA.

The Class visited the old Moorish palace at Cintra,—Cintra, on whose flower-crowned peaks, the Portuguese poet says, Spring sits enthroned. The arabesque ornaments on the exterior of the castle of Pintra at Cintra began to reveal to the boys the beauties of Moorish art, which were to excite their admiration in all their journeys through Portugal and Spain.

Who were the Moors? The race will be constantly spoken of in the zigzag journey through Spain. It is a term that the new reader of Spanish history sometimes fails to understand.

The Moors of to-day are the inhabitants of Barbary, or the States of Morocco, Algiers, Tunis, and Tripoli, in Northern Africa. The Moors of Spanish history were Arabs, or Saracens. These conquered the people of

Northern Africa and converted them to the Mahometan faith in the eighth century. The Arabs having resolved to make a conquest of Spain summoned the Moors to help them, and the whole army of the invaders was called *Moors*. These conquered a large portion of Spain, and founded the romantic Kingdom of Granada. The Moors were at last expelled from Spain, when they established piratical governments in Algiers, Tunis, and Morocco.

The Class made but one long excursion from Lisbon. It was to Coimbra, the seat of one of the oldest universities in Europe.

The town is built on a conical hill, and is surrounded by olive gardens and orange groves, and unites the loveliness of Nature to the charm of antiquity. The university has about one thousand students, many of them being from Brazil.

Coimbra was built by the Goths, conquered by the Moors, and the Moors were expelled from it by the CID.

Who was the Cid?

THE STORY OF THE CID.

In Spain chivalry means honor, and is deemed life's crowning virtue; and the most brilliant illustration of chivalry, or what a true knight should be, is found in the life and character of the Cid.

Spain is full of Cid romances, for the Cid in Spanish poetry is made to illustrate every virtue of a true knight; and poets continued to relate new exploits of the model hero of Spain, long after the Campeador (or Champion), as he was called, had turned to dust.

When one wished to illustrate what a true man should be, he told some marvellous story of virtue and valor and attributed it to the Cid. If the Cid could rise from his splendid tomb, we fancy he would be more astonished at the improvements in his own biography than at the engine winding its swift way through his native mountains.

The favorite ballad of Spain is "The Cid." The favorite stage-play of the Middle Ages was "The Cid." The finest old songs of the Spanish peninsula relate to the Cid.

Rodrigo Diaz, the Cid Campeador, or Lord Champion, was born at Burgos, about the year 1025.

When he was a mere boy his father was insulted by a powerful nobleman, the Count of Gomez; Rodrigo took a sword, strode forth in fierce anger and cut off the count's head. He carried the head of the impolite count to his father, saying,—

"Well have I avenged thee, father!
Well have sped me in the fight;
For to him is vengeance certain,
Who doth arm himself with right."

This is very good poetry, and it was a very fine thing for the noble Cid to say; but boys now-a-days would hardly be expected to dispose of unmannerly people in just that way.

TABLEAU OF "THE CID" IN THE MIDDLE AGES.

The impolite count left a daughter, named Ximena; and she thought it rather impolite in the Cid to kill her father, and so endeavored to induce the king to kill *him*. But the Cid soon after conquered five Moorish chiefs, and his valor so filled the changeful Ximena with admiration that she said to King Ferdinand, one day,—

"I have a request to make."
"Name it."
"That you will give me in marriage to the Cid."
"It shall be as you wish."

They had a great wedding for those times. This is the way the bridegroom was dressed: his pants were fringed with purple; his shoes were scarlet; he had on a "*slashed* leathern jacket," — slashed in memory of his many slashes in the field, and possibly of the slashes he had given the lovely bride's father; his cloak was plush, and he had a cock's feather in his cap; and, take it all in all, he must have looked very interesting indeed.

And the lovely Ximena? She had a fine "gown of London cloth," and "two *flaps*" over her ears, and a "*flap*" on her back, whatever that may be; she walked on "high-heeled clogs of red leather," and her necklace was "worth a whole city."

As she passed along in her high-heeled boots there were great rejoicings, fine music, and strewings of flowers. At the wedding dinner the Cid gave a jester the enormous sum of about five cents "because he scared the women so well."

The Cid was so honest that the king banished him as quick as a Congress or Legislature taboos a very honest man to-day. He submitted very gracefully, however, —

>"I obey, O King Alfonso!
>Guilty though in nought I be;
>For it doth behoove a vassal
>To obey a lord's decree."

But he proved such a valiant warrior in exile that he was soon restored to the royal favor.

The Cid had two daughters, from whom are supposed to be descended the proud royal families of Aragon and Castile. They were wedded to the Count of Barcelona and the Infant of Navarre. The weddings took place at Valencia, and were even finer than the Cid's own. They had bull-fights for eight days, which must have been indeed an edifying spectacle for the brides. The Cid made splendid wedding presents, —

>"He who is great in deeds of battle
>Will be great in all beside."

But the counts who had won the Cid's daughter were sad cowards.

They were sitting in the Cid's palace one day, when a lion broke loose from his cage and rushed into the room.

>"So loud outcries rent the palace,
>Shook its walls and turrets high!
>''Ware the lion! 'ware the lion!
>He is loose!' was heard the cry."

The two counts heard the cry "'Ware the lion!" and "'ware the lion" they did. One darted under the table and the other rushed into the wine-press. The Cid was asleep; the confusion awoke him. He took the lion by the mane and led him to the cage. Then he gave the two counts the following magnificent reproval: —

> "Had ye not your weapons with you?
> Why then fled ye in such haste?
> Was the Cid not here? then surely
> Ye could stand and see the beast!"

But stories of the Cid would fill a dozen books like this. He fought in many battles for Spain. He died in Valencia in 1099. His dead body clad like a knight was carried on horseback to the Convent of Cardena, where it was clothed in cloth of gold, and Ximena sang masses for the soul. It was buried before the altar.

At Coimbra the class visited the castle, now in ruins, where Inez de Castro lived, and the garden in which she was murdered.

THE STORY OF INEZ DE CASTRO.

Dom Pedro was the son of Alphonso IV., a monarch of stern and inflexible disposition, whose word was law and whose presence was terror. Dom Pedro was a handsome prince. He was married early in life to Constanzia, a noble lady, and a suitable spouse to the heir of the bright-skied kingdom.

Constanzia had a maid of honor who was a descendant of one of the noblest and richest families of Gallacia. She was a cousin of the queen.

If we were to believe the old writers, Inez de Castro was one of the most enchanting beauties the world has ever seen. The prince became enamored of her, and lost his regard for the stately and high-minded Constanzia. When the latter found that her radiant cousin had won the prince's affections, she became melancholy, and died of a broken heart (1344).

The prince, at an uncertain date after this event, married Inez de Castro. The marriage was secret; it was not legalized for a number of years.

Dom Pedro, much as in the case of Henry II. and Fair Rosamond, selected a secluded spot for the residence of his bride, and he devoted himself with a remarkable fondness almost exclusively to her society.

The courtiers, jealous of the house of Castro, reported to grim King Alphonso his son's fondness for Inez. Alphonso was immediately seized with a suspicion and fear that the beautiful woman would use her boundless influence over the prince to set aside the claims of the son of his late true queen, Constanzia, and seek to elevate her own child to the succession to the throne.

Alphonso persuaded himself that the stability of the royal house and the kingdom demanded the removal of Inez de Castro from her position of influence and power.

One day Dom Pedro went hunting, intending to be absent from his family for a few days, as was his wont when leading a grand hunting-party. Inez with her children retired to the Convent of St. Clair, at Coimbra, to pass her time in devotion, possibly thinking that such acts of piety would atone for the receiving the prince's affection before their marriage, when his wife was pining for sorrow.

Suddenly, Alphonso appeared at the convent and demanded an immediate interview with Inez.

The summons struck her to the heart. She knew its import; she threw herself before him and implored him to spare her life.

The sight of her wonderful beauty and of her innocent children for the moment softened him. He retired from her presence; but soon after returning to his original purpose, which was to murder her, he gave an order to some secret assassins to do the deed.

There was a beautiful garden at Coimbra, which is now called "The Garden of Tears." There Inez was sitting, anxiously awaiting her husband's return, when some dark-visaged men came creeping into the bowers. They rushed upon her and struck her dead (1355). The so-called stain of her blood on a stone is still shown in the delightful garden.

Dom Pedro hurried to the convent on returning from the chase, expecting to receive the kisses of his wife and children. When he found Inez murdered and his children gone, he was seized with a melancholy madness, and to revenge the death of Inez became the sole purpose of his life.

Alphonso, after the tragedy, became a prey to remorse, which ended untimely his days. He died 1357.

Pedro ascended the throne, the fire of revenge still unquenched within him.

He first sought out the assassins of Inez. One of these had escaped to Aragon, and the other to Castile. He secured them, and caused them to be placed in a dungeon where they could hear the rushing of a stream of water, but could receive none to quench their burning thirst. When they were nearly wasted with hunger, they were put to the torture of the taxello and capello, to the rack and pincers; and, after having their bones pulled apart and their muscles torn away, were at last cast into the fire, and their ashes thrown to the wind. This all seems to be a terrible and unjust punishment, for the men did only what they were ordered to do by the king.

INTERIOR OF THE CATHEDRAL, SEVILLE

He next convoked an assembly of the representatives of the States, and established before them the proof of his marriage with Inez.

The body of Inez was taken from its grave by his order, and dressed in the most magnificent robes, jewelled, and put upon a throne. The dead queen was then crowned, with all the pomp of royalty.

> "A peal of lordly music
> Shook e'en the dust below,
> As the burning gold of the diadem
> Was placed on her pallid brow."

She was buried with royal ceremonies at Alcobaça. The king and lords of Portugal followed her remains on foot to the final resting-place, a distance of sixty miles. A splendid monument was there raised to her memory; and Camoens, the great poet of Portugal, has celebrated the romantic story in the "Lusiad." Mrs. Hemans has vividly pictured in verse the scene of the crowning of the dead queen, and the subject has been treated by Spanish and other writers of tragedy.

From Lisbon the Class went to Badajos by rail, a distance of about one hundred and seventy-five miles. On the route, at Santarem, the church was seen in which lie the remains of Dom Pedro Alvares Cabral, the discoverer of Brazil. This town is very ancient, the *Præ-sidium Julium* of Latin history.

"I shall put down the town as 'Zag' in my note-book," said Tommy Toby. "Lisbon was 'Zig,' and this must be 'Zag,' for we are now zig-zagging through the old Roman Empire."

At Badajos the Class visited the cathedral, begun in 1248, and saw in the Capilla Santa Ana some grim pictures by Morales. This painter was born at Badajos, and a street here bears his name. Philip II. visited him in 1581.

"You are very old, Morales," said the king.

"And very poor," replied the poet.

The hint had its effect. The king made Morales a pensioner for life.

The Class decided to make their next journey, to Seville, on horseback. Tommy Toby strongly favored this plan.

"You will traverse La Florida," said a muleteer.

"Which means we shall ride through flower-land," said Tommy, "and on horseback. I hope the journey will be a long one."

"It will be long enough," said Master Lewis; "and I think that your wish will be fully gratified before we arrive at the first inn."

The Class were to follow the lead of a party of muleteers and carriers, — gay, light-hearted fellows, who could tell wonderful stories, and whose conversation was much spiced with jokes, repartee, and scraps of song.

The boys had English saddles and spurs, and felt as chivalrous as Don Quixote. Outside of Badajos the air was all fragrance, and the pastures all bloom. The mules trotted along with a queer, half-reluctant gait, which seemed to imply that they must feel the prick of the spur in order to *go*. Some of them were laden with a peculiar kind of basket made of Spanish grass, divided into two parts, filled with food and travelling necessities.

A few hours' ride brought the party to La Albuera, the old battle-ground in the Spanish campaign of Napoleon's marshal, Soult, in 1811.

"We have now come fifteen miles," said a muleteer.

"*Fifteen* miles!" said Tommy; "I thought we had ridden an hundred."

The sun was burning fiercely; Tommy's face began to wear a most distressed expression.

"How much longer shall we have to ride in *this* way?" he asked, in an earnest tone.

"You said you hoped the journey would be a long one," said Master Lewis. "It is only begun. How do you feel?"

"My legs feel like two sticks of wood. The heat is dreadful, and every *zig* is a little worse than the other *zag*."

Tommy referred to the motion of the horse.

At distances of about fifteen miles they came to little Spanish

HALL OF THE AMBASSADORS, SEVILLE.

towns, where they met with a cordial welcome at the posada, as the country inn is called.

The country all along the way was full of rich pastures, fat pigs and sheep, and very miserable-looking peasants.

"All kinds of flowers seem to bloom in Spain," said Wyllys.

"Except the flower of civilization," said Master Lewis.

The inns where the party stopped for the night were clean and cool, though very simple in their furnishing. Tommy said they used rocks for pillows.

At a village called El Ronquillo the party were entertained by a story of a grim Alcalde who was born there, and who entered the service of Charles V.

"He made it a point to execute all whom he arrested," said the muleteer. "He always killed the aged."

The muleteer paused.

"Why?" asked Master Lewis.

"For what they *had* done. And he always executed the young."

Another pause.

"Why?" asked Master Lewis.

"For what they *might* do."

Seville, a city of one hundred and twenty-five thousand inhabitants, at last rose before the dusty and weary travellers; and the very name seemed to the Class like a charm and inspiration. Seville, the Romula or Little Rome of Cæsar! Seville, the marvel of Andalusia! Seville, once enriched with spoils of the golden isles of the deep!

"I am glad this journey is coming to an end," said Tommy. "I hope we may never make another such an one."

"It makes one feel like Æneas," said Master Lewis.

"Why like Æneas?" asked Tommy.

"He was much 'tossed about by land as well as by sea.'"

Seville lies on the bank of the Gaudalquiver, and is enclosed by Moorish walls. It has been thought to exceed any other city in the world in poetry and beauty. " Those who have not seen Seville have not seen a wonder," is a Spanish proverb. "Springtime in Andalusia" has been used to express the perfection of earthly beauty, and springtime in Seville has a charm that few spots in the world can equal.

The Class took lodgings at the Fond de Londres, a fine commercial inn. The balconies of the boys' rooms looked out on the Plasa, which was fragrant with orange trees. The first visit was to the cathedral.

This structure is the glory of Seville and the pride of Spain. The architect of this amazing monument of beauty is unknown; he seems not to have thought of himself, but only of God, in his work. What visions and dreams must have passed before his fancy as he mapped out the plan!

The centre nave is magnificent, and its height is bewildering, one hundred and seventy-one feet. The cupola seems to be suspended in air, as though held in position by some miraculous power. The grandeur of the interior is stern and overpowering; the painted windows seem more than an earthly glory, and the walls are adorned with the matchless pictures of Murillo.

Alcaza, the old palace of the Moorish kings, but still resplendent with gold and a wealth of color, was next sought. It was like a fabulous building, with its numberless arabesques, its mosaics, its variegated woods, its porcelain decorations, its slender but graceful marble columns.

"I should imagine the days of Haroun-al-Raschid had come again," said Tommy.

"Evidently wood-carving was understood before the invention of the jig-saw," he added drolly, gazing in wonder on the superb doors and windows.

"Almost as fine as your carvings at Yuleville," said Master Lewis.

"Yes, 't is very good work," said Tommy, "considering it was done by *heathen* Moors."

The garden was as wonderful in its beauty as the palace. The trees and flower-beds were so trimmed and had so been made to grow as to represent other forms of beauty, — crowns, maps, shafts, monuments. The walks were amid wonderful fountains, the water being made to bubble up amid the stones, and grottoes and arbors like fairyland. Seville was the birthplace of

MURILLO.

Here he lived; and here, in the Gallery of Art, four-and-twenty of his memorable paintings are to be seen.

He was born in 1618. He was an orphan and poor, but his passion for art began almost in the cradle, and early grew into a fixed purpose in life; and unknown to any one he left his home and set out for Madrid, where lived Valasquez. This great master gave him a home in his house, and became his foster-father; and from that hour his fame, that was to fill the world, began.

The pictures of Murillo have a charm like enchantment; they have a warmth like life, and a glow as of celestial beauty. Every art-loving eye in the world is familiar with copies of Murillo's Madonna.

Antonio Castillo y Saavedra, of Cordova, believed himself to be the finest painter of his time. He visited Seville, and saw some of the pictures of Murillo.

"It is all over with Castillo," he said.

When he found his own genius so greatly surpassed, he is said to have died of disappointment at the failure of his own ambition to be the first painter in Spain.

Over the altar in the parish church where Murillo worshipped was a famous picture of the Descent from the Cross by a Flemish artist. Day by day Murillo was seen to linger before it.

"Why do you tarry so long before that picture?" one asked.

"I am waiting for those men to bring the body of the Blessed Lord down the ladder."

Beneath this altar his body was buried with almost regal pomp.

The Class went from Seville to Granada by diligence over an excellent and picturesque road, full of shade and fragrance and views of Moorish ruins, a distance of one hundred and forty-six miles.

CHAPTER VI.

THROUGH THE HEART OF SPAIN.

GRANADA. — THE ALHAMBRA. — THE STORY OF THE ABENCERRAGES. — MADRID. — TOMMY TOBY SEES A BULL-FIGHT. — SARAGOSSA. — THE STORY OF THE CHRISTENING OF QUEEN MARY'S BABY.

T was April, one of the most beautiful months of the year in Southern Spain. Everywhere was felt the charm of pure skies, glowing sunshine, and delicious airs; of the fragrance of valleys of verdure and hills of bloom. The snows on the sides of the Sierra Nevada were melting, and pouring through all the land their glorious streams.

The plain on which Granada is situated is said to be the loveliest in the world. Springtime brings to it its crowning enchantment. It was once believed by the Moors that Valencia lay on the very borders of Paradise, and in springtime one is persuaded to believe that he sees in Granada as well a land emparadised in beauty and bloom. The goddess Flora might have here made her palace. It is said that the nightingales sing here all the year.

The plain is watered by the River Xenil. On the east runs the River Darro through the orchards and olive gardens of the so-called Valley of Paradise. Always in sight rise the mountains skirted with blossoms of every hue and crowned with eternal snow.

The Class took lodgings in the Fonda de l'Alamada, and afterwards in a hotel near the palace of the Alhambra, named in honor of Washington Irving. Almost the first walks that the Class made

COURT OF THE LIONS.

was to that most romantic palace of all the world's palaces, the Alhambra.

The palace stands on a high hill between the Xenil and Darro, and in the days of Moorish glory it was a fortress as well as royal seat.

The description of this palace would fill volumes. An Arab poet has exceeded all other writers in his delineation of its matchless beauty. He makes it to say: "*My pillars were brought from Eden, my garden is the Paradise; of hewn jewels are my walls, and my ceilings are dyed with the hues of the wings of angels. I was paved with petrified flowers, and those who see me laugh and sing. My columns are blocks of pearl by night; by day, perpetual sunshine turns my fountains to gold.*"

This is Oriental hyperbole, but the palace is a marvel of art and architectural illusion. The clustering columns seem so light as to have no stability; ingenious arabesques in wonderful contrasts of color, interlaced with every spiral and line of beauty that can charm the eye, are seen on every hand. These columns, which are of marble, jasper, and porphyry, support roofs that gleam with gold and mother-of-pearl. The halls are full of basins, streams, and fountains, which give a delightful coolness to the air.

The principal halls are called the Hall of Lions, the Hall of the Ambassadors, and the Abencerrages. The Moors said of the Court of the Lions, so called from the figures of twelve lions which support the fountain: "*Here is a garden containing wonders of art which God forbids should elsewhere be found.*"

A LEGEND.

The halls, courts, and gardens of the Alhambra abound in the associations of legends and stories which the Class had read, and which they rehearsed here; but we must refer the reader to the works of Irving and Prescott, and to Miss Yonge's "Christians and Moors of Spain," for them. The hall which has the most tragic legend is that of the Abencerrages. These people were one of the noblest races of the Moors. They had a feud with another high-born family or race of the Moors, called the Zegris. The latter were in favor with the king and court.

The Zegris persuaded the king to murder the Abencerrages, and he summoned them to the beautiful palace, and had them admitted to the airy and fantastic hall that bears their name. In the Hall of the Lions, of which we give a picture, a band of Zegris was stationed with an executioner.

FOUNTAIN IN THE ALHAMBRA.

A page went out of this hall and summoned one of the Abencerrages. Only one.

He obeyed. As the door closed after him he was seized, and was beheaded over a huge vase of alabaster.

Then another was summoned.

He shared the same fate.

Another.

One by one, until thirty-five had been killed.

GENERAL VIEW OF THE ALHAMBRA.

A page chanced to follow one of the doomed men to the door, and he discovered the horrible work that was going on. He managed to escape, and gave the alarm. The friends of the Abencerrages raised a force of soldiers, who immediately began to slaughter the Zegris. When Alhama, one of the strong towns that protected Granada, was conquered by the Christians, the loss was attributed to the judgment of Heaven for the murder of the Abencerrages, and it was prophesied that the Alhambra itself would soon fall.

> The Moorish King rides up and down
> Through Granada's royal town;
> From Elvira's gates to those
> Of Vivarambla on he goes.
> > Woe is me, Alhama!
>
> Letters to the monarch tell
> How Alhama's city fell:
> In the fire the scroll he threw,
> And the messenger he slew.
> > Woe is me, Alhama!
>
> He quits his mule and mounts his horse,
> And through the street directs his course:
> Through the street of Zacatin,
> To the Alhambra spurring in.
> > Woe is me, Alhama!
>
> When the Alhambra walls he gained,
> On the moment he ordain'd
> That the trumpet straight should sound
> With the silver clarion round.
> > ·Woe is me, Alhama!
>
> And when the hollow drums of war
> Beat the loud alarm afar,
> That the Moors of town and plain
> Might answer to the martial strain,
> > Woe is me, Alhama!
>
> Then the Moors, by this aware
> That bloody Mars recall'd them there,
> One by one, and two by two,
> To a mighty squadron grew.
> > Woe is me, Alhama!

Out then spake an aged Moor
In these words the king before :
"Wherefore call on us, O King?
What may mean this gathering?"
    Woe is me, Alhama!

"Friends, ye have, alas! to know
Of a most disastrous blow ;
That the Christians, stern and bold,
Have obtained Alhama's hold."
    Woe is me, Alhama!

Out then spake old Alfaqui,
With his beard so white to see :
"Good King! thou art justly served ;
Good King! this hast thou deserved.
    Woe is me, Alhama!

By thee were slain, in evil hour,
The Abencerrage, Grenada's flower ;
And strangers were received by thee
Of Cordova the Chivalry.
    Woe is me, Alhama!

And for this, O King! is sent
On thee a double chastisement :
Thee and thine, thy crown and realm,
One last wreck shall overwhelm.
    Woe is me, Alhama!

He who holds no laws in awe,
He must perish by the law ;
And Granada must be won,
And thyself with her undone."
    Woe is me, Alhama!

When this prophecy was fulfilled and Granada was taken, it is said that the last Moorish king — the unlucky Boabdil — wept as the city, with its countless beauties and glorious Alhambra, vanished out of his sight, and he wound his way along the mountain pass that led towards the sea. It was the end of perhaps the most romantic and poetic kingdom the world has ever seen.

CAVE DWELLING OF THE GYPSIES.

The Class made several interesting excursions outside of the city of Granada. One of these was to the cave-dwellings of the gypsies, or habitations made in the sides of the hills. Here they saw a race of

AN OLD GYPSY.

thievish men, jockeys; fortune-telling hags, withered, with bright crafty eyes; handsome young women with castinets, and children in swarms almost destitute of clothing.

As they were riding in a diligence on one of these excursions, towards nightfall they passed an old musician, evidently a gypsy, who played very sweetly on the guitar, and used his utmost efforts to attract their attention. But no money was thrown out to him. As the diligence rolled on, he was seen to throw his arms into the air, as in great distress and despair.

"I wish I could meet him again," said Wyllys, touched by his attitude, which was at once comic and pathetic.

A long journey of two hundred and seventy-four miles, chiefly by rail, took the Class through wild mountain scenery, valleys of pomegranites and figs, beautiful hills clad with vineyards and old Moorish-looking towns, to Madrid, the capital of Spain.

Madrid has a population of three hundred and twenty thousand, a much smaller number than Granada in the times of the Moors. It is built on a loftly plateau, and is cooled by the currents of air that flow down from the peaks of the Guadarrama.

The Class took lodgings in a private house, as it was cheaper, paying about thirty reals (real 2½d.) per day. The houses are very tall, and different families live in many flats of the same house, using the staircase as a common thoroughfare.

The Class at Madrid went to the Royal Palace, which they did not enter, and made an excursion out of the city to the Escurial, the intended Versailles of Spain, a palace in a desert place, the old and present burial-place of Spanish kings. It was begun by Philip II., who made a vow it is said, during battle, that he would build a monastery to St. Lawrence, if God would give him the victory. St. Lawrence suffered martyrdom by being roasted on a gridiron; and the palace is built in the form of a gridiron, in fulfilment of the vow. It is seven hundred feet long and five hundred and sixty-four wide, and is second only in size and solidity to the Pyramids of Egypt. The Pantheon, or chamber of dead kings, is perhaps the most solemn and gorgeous tomb in the world. The walls are of jasper and precious stones. It contains twenty-six sarcophagi.

BULL-FIGHT.

THE BULL-FIGHT.

A few days after the arrival of the Class at Madrid, there was to be a bull-fight on Monday. There had been a bull-fight at Seville while the Class was there, but it took place on Sunday.

"All the city are going to the fight," said Tommy to Master Lewis; "are you not going?"

"On Sunday?"

"The same people who attended mass in the morning, at least all of those at our hotel, are going," said Tommy; "and I heard an Englishman say that probably a priest would be present to hear confession, in case any one in the ring should be killed."

"There is a true morality in the world," said Master Lewis, "and there is a conventional morality. By a conventional morality I mean an acceptance of custom as the rule of duty, or 'doing' as we say, 'among Romans as Romans do.' If it is right for me to go to the bull-fight this afternoon, it would be perfectly proper for me to go to a horse-race or a dog-fight in America on a Sunday afternoon, if anything so disgraceful were possible in our country."

"But you will go with us before we leave Spain?" said Tommy.

"To a *bull-fight?*"

"Why not? we came to foreign lands to see what we could see. The great English gentlemen and the fine French people all go. See the carriages leaving the hotel!"

"Do you wish to see maddened bulls disembowel helpless horses?" asked Master Lewis.

"Nearly all the kings and queens of Spain, since the Cid, as I have read, have held it to be a manly sport."

"I believe it originated with the Moors," said Master Lewis, — "a people noted for their cruelty. Good Queen Isabella, the patron of Columbus, tried to abolish the custom, but found the depraved taste of the people too strong for her influence. Pizarro, as you may suppose, was a champion bull-fighter, as were all the bloody Philipses. See the effect of all this cruelty on the national character. Did you never read about the old Spanish Inquisition and the Auto da fé?"

"No, not carefully. But I have always loved to read hunting-stories in American papers, and I have often thought I would like to see animals fight. It is but carrying out their instincts."

"The bulls that are to fight the horses in the arena to-day have probably been kept without food a long time, and are burning with thirst. As soon as they enter the ring they will be tortured, in order to madden them. They would not be likely to attack the horses in their own pastures, and, if they were so disposed, the horses would be able to use their natural defence, — superior speed."

"True," said Tommy.

"What you say about your reading," said Master Lewis, "only shows the pernicious effect of a certain kind of stories which are too common in American publications for young people, — stories of hunting animals for sport. They stimulate brutal passions, as they have yours, through the imagination. The old 'bird's-nest commandment' of the Bible has lost its force in modern boys' books. I have almost as much respect for a saloon keeper as for an author the influence of whose writings leads to cruelty to the dumb, helpless, brute creation. The truly great and good have always been kind to harmless animals. One thing that makes me respect the Hindus is that they scrupulously protect every animal, that is itself harmless, from being molested."

At Madrid, Tommy had been allowed by Master Lewis to visit the places he liked with sons of an English gentleman whose acquaintance he had made, and, not having been explicitly forbidden to do so, he accepted their invitation to go with him to the bull-fight.

There are twenty-four bull-fights at Madrid every year. From April to October they are given on Sundays or Mondays. The one of which we are about to speak was given on Monday. The Plasa de Toros, where these exhibitions take place, will hold sixteen thousand people. It is about a mile and a half from the centre of Madrid, and on the borders of one of those wild, desolate-looking regions that lie in view of the city and make one wonder at its strange situation. It is reached by an avenue bordered at first by elegant villas, then by forges, slaughter-houses, and queer work-shops.

Through this avenue all the people of the city seemed pouring like a flood. Lords and ladies in elegant equipages, brown Andalusians, beggars, gypsies, muleteers, idlers, the young and old, as though the fate of the city were staked on the result of the contest.

Tommy and his English friends were borne along by this motley concourse like boats on the tide, their wonder and excitement growing at every step. They were able to obtain standing room only, and this among a wild crowd of men and boys near the ring of the arena.

"I have been told," said one of the English boys, "that this corridor is a very dangerous place. Suppose the bull should leap over the barrier!"

"He could not do it," said Tommy: "it is too high."

THE ROYAL PALACE, MADRID.

"But I have read that the bull often leaps into the first corridor, and when he does so, and scatters the spectators, there is great fun and laughter in the amphitheatre."

Suddenly the trumpets sounded a fanfare, and the gates to the arena were opened. There entered a glittering cavalcade, that looked like a picture of the days of chivalry. First came the masters of ceremonies dressed in black, and mounted on proud and prancing steeds. Then followed heralds sounding bugles, and behind them the protectors of the toreadors, or bull-fighters, in splendid costumes. These were gentlemen of noble birth. The picadores or spearmen came next, with jackets glittering with silver; then footmen in purple and green; then the espaders in silken attire bedecked with gold, with blood-red cloaks on their arms, and a well-tempered sword in their right hands with which to give the animal his death-thrust. The procession closed with mules adorned with plumes and tinkling with bells. These were to carry away the dead animals.

The cavalcade went round the circle and stopped in front of a throne-like balcony. The sunlight fell upon the arena, on the gay and excited multitude, the splendid dresses, the waving fans. The gates were again opened, and a magnificent bull bounded into the ring.

The light, the gay throng, the blare of the music, seemed to confuse him. He stopped and looked around, as though he would be glad to get away. The banderilleros tried to tease him with their red capes, and the picadores brandished their lances; the poor horses, each with one eye bound up that he might not have a full view of his adversary and become frightened, wheeled hither and thither, — but the bull seemed reluctant to make an attack.

"I would like to pull his tail," said Tommy, "and see him *go*."

A little fellow sprang directly in front of the bull, holding a bright-red cloak before the animal's eyes. The bull made a lunge at it, but the nimble fellow moved aside with a sort of dancing gait, and the animal met only the resistance of the fluttering folds. This maddened him. He turned in an instant upon one of the poor half-blind horses, and drove his horns into the animal's body. The horse was next seen plunging around the arena dragging his entrails on the ground.

"What a horrible sight!" said one of the English boys. "I hope I may never see the like again. I wish I had not come. I wish all those people in the arena could be struck ——"

Above there was a great shouting, all the people seeming to be in a fervor of pleasurable excitement. The wounded horse fell, raised his head quivering in agony, ran out his tongue, and died.

The bull turned upon a cape-bearer, who came nimbly leaping over the barrier into the very circle where the boys were.

"Suppose the bull were to follow him?" queried Tommy.

There was a great shout in the amphitheatre; bouquets were flying through the air. The bull was lying on the sand, his eyes rolling back in his head. An espader had dealt him a deadly thrust with his sword, and the blood was flowing from the wound in jets.

"Viva! viva! viva!" shouted thousands of voices.

There was soon another sound of trumpets. Another bull came rushing in, tearing up the earth at every bound. He rushed immediately upon a horse and disembowelled him, then upon another. He scattered the cape-bearers like a flock of birds. His rage was terrible to look upon.

Suddenly he paused, and the foam fell from his mouth. Then he lifted his head, ran towards the barrier where the boys were standing, and with one fearful bound cleared the wall, and was dashing about the corridor.

The boys were filled with terror, expecting to be attacked and gored, and perhaps sent flying into the arena. The men in the corridor leaped into the arena, excited, but laughing as though it was an expected thing. The English boys followed their example. Tommy attempted to do the same, but the bull gave a fearful snort just as he reached the top of the barrier, and he rolled over into the arena in a most comical way. Being a foreigner, and exhibiting in his face his terror, he became the object on which all eyes were fixed.

"Go home and bury yourself!" shouted a voice in Spanish. There was a great roar of laughter.

In a moment the people who had leaped out of the corridor were climbing back again. The English boys and Tommy followed. The bull was being driven back through the gates into the arena.

"Allow us to pass out," said one of the English boys to the state official or *gendarme*, and that gentleman at a convenient interval of the shocking proceedings allowed the boys to leave the place.

"I never want to get into such a place as that again," said Tommy.

"We will say nothing about this at the hotel," said one of the English boys.

"I won't, if you won't," said Tommy.

"How would you like to pull *his* tail now, just to see him go?"

"I saw him *go*," said Tommy, "and *they* saw me go. I guess Master Lewis is right about bull-fighting."

From Madrid the Class went to Saragossa, the capital of the old kingdom of Aragon. It is a picturesque city when viewed from the distance, but much of the charm is lost on entering it, as its streets are narrow, and its buildings decayed. It has a leaning tower like Pisa, which is of Moorish origin, and a very beautiful monument of Moorish art.

The pride of Saragossa is its cathedral, which the people believe to have been founded by St. James and to have been visited by the Virgin, attended with one thousand angels.

We will relate a story of Aragon, which will give the reader a view of the manners and customs and religious habits of the old-time court and of the people to-day.

STORY OF CHRISTENING QUEEN MARY'S BABY.

Santiago, or St. James, is the patron saint of Spain, and among all the names of the twelve apostles his is there held in the highest esteem.

The people of Aragon believe that St. James applied to the Virgin Mary for permission to preach the gospel in Spain. Having obtained her consent, he kissed her hand, and started for Saragossa, where he was the means of the conversion of eight pagans. In 40 A. D., January 2, — the date is very exactly given, — the angels brought the Virgin from Palestine on a jasper pillar, and she desired St. James to build a church on the spot where the pillar rested. Hence arose the wonderful shrine of Aragon, the Chapel of the Pillar, which is a part of a cathedral whose clustering domes and parti-colored roofs present a scene of Oriental magnificence.

Although the date is so exact, the story itself seems to admit of some variation. We are told that the Virgin used to come from paradise to attend mass at the chapel, and that she descended on this very pillar.

This pillar is the pride, hope, and consolation of the people of Saragossa. It is regarded as too sacred wholly to be seen by common eyes; only priests and kings are admitted into its immediate sanctuary: women are prohibited. Innumerable miracles have been supposed to be wrought at the shrine, even to the making whole of an amputated leg. On the anniversary of the descent of the Virgin from heaven, October 12, as many as fifty thousand pilgrims have been known to enter the town.

But we began to tell an amusing story, and amusing stories are rare under the sun of Spain, notwithstanding that "Don Quixote" had its origin there. Humor belongs to the Northern lands, and tragedy and passion to the soil of the South. Aragon is full of tragedies, but is poor in cheerful fireside-tales.

Mary was Queen of Aragon, and the dearest wish of her heart was that she might bear a son, to be heir to the kingdom.

This was her first wish. Her second wish was that the heir might be named James.

> "The second wish of Queen Mary's heart
> Is to have that son called James,
> Because she thought for the Spanish king
> 'Twas the best of all good names."

Now Queen Mary had prayed to *all* the twelve apostles for an heir, and when a son was born to her she did not herself dare to give him the name of James, lest in so doing she should offend the other eleven apostles, whom she supposed had been equally gracious in answering her prayer.

She was greatly troubled what to do.

She sent for her confessor, good Bishop Boyl.

"The apostles have all been good to me, and I wish to give my son the name of one of them. Since I cannot give him the name of all the twelve, which shall I choose?"

"Procure twelve tapers," said the bishop. "Let them be of the same size and weight, and name them for the twelve apostles."

"And then —"

"Light them, and the one that burns the longest shall give the name to the child."

The nuns made the twelve candles, and the holy fathers blessed them and twelve golden candlesticks, and put into the twelve candlesticks the twelve tapers bearing the names of the twelve apostles.

The twelve candlesticks were placed on twelve altars, and beside the twelve altars stood twelve priests.

The ladies of the queen, with their rosaries in their hands, came to pray during the burning of the tapers; and the chief men of the kingdom assembled in the hall of state to await the decision of the lights.

Then all the twelve tapers were lighted at the same time.

The women all began to count their beads, and the priests all began to pray.

The queen lay on her bed of state, watching the lights, with her child near her.

THE LEANING TOWER OF SARAGOSSA.

St. Peter was the first to burn out.
Presently St. John was gone.
Then St. Matthias expired.
Then St. Matthew.
St. Andrew.
St. Philip.
St. Bartholomew.

The queen suddenly began to look wild and anxious.

A startling thought had come to her.

Suppose the lot should fall upon St. JUDAS, the second disciple of that name! King Judas!!

She grew greatly troubled.

Judas was burning most slowly of all. The sight of it made the queen shudder.

St. Simon turned to ashes.

Then St. Thomas.

But Judas stood tall and bright, and seemed hardly consumed at all.

There were only three tapers remaining, — the dreadful Judas and the two Saints James.

St. James the Less presently expired.

There were but two left now, — St. James the lover of Spain, and St. Judas.

Suddenly there was a gutter in the taper of St. James, and it began to carry away the wax in a stream.

The queen was now in despair.

She started up and cried, —

"I never will call him *Judas!* It is not a Christian name."

But Judas stood tall and bright, and James was going out.

"Holy Mother, preserve us!" groaned the queen.

"Holy Mother, preserve us!" groaned the priests.

"Holy Mother, preserve us!" groaned every one.

Even the infant began to cry.

Just then a moth flew in at the window.

It fluttered around St. Judas.

James fell in the socket, but was still burning.

It was going out —

The moth dashed its wings against Judas.

It was extinguished!

Then James flamed up, and, amid the *glorias* of the queen, priests, and court, slowly expired.

"Oh that was joy for Queen Mary's heart!
 The babe was christened James;
The Prince of Aragon hath got
 The best of all good names.

"Glory to Santiago,
 The mighty one in war!
James he is called, and he shall be
 King James the Conqueror!

"Shine higher now, ye stars that crown
 Our Lady del Pilar!
And rejoice in thy grave, Cid Campeador,
 Ruy Diaz de Bivar!"

If the reader would know more of the history of James, we would refer him to Miss Yonge's "Story of the Christians and Moors of Spain."

The Class now journeyed towards the sea, and reached Barcelona — once the place of the old Spanish Inquisition, but now the chief commercial city of the kingdom — on the 1st of May. From Barcelona the Class sailed for Marseilles.

CHAPTER VII.

MARSEILLES AND THE RHONE.

MARSEILLES. — STORY OF THE MARSEILLAISE HYMN. — OTHER MEMBERS OF THE ZIGZAG CLUB TO JOIN THE EXCURSION. — THE RHONE. — THE PLAGUE AT MARSEILLES. — AN UNEXPECTED ARRIVAL. — THE STORY OF THE CRUSADES OF THE CHILDREN.

N arriving at Marseilles, the Class took rooms at the Grand Hotel.

What a series of interesting historical pictures pass before the mind of the reader of history at the sound and sight of Marseilles!

Marseilles, the fair Ionian City, the sister of Tyre, graced with elegant temples and enlivened with the gay festivals of Diana! Marseilles, the adopted daughter of Rome, the friend of Pompey, the foe of imperialism under the reign of the Cæsars, the advocate of liberty when all the world was governed by one crown! Marseilles, that gave a home to Milo, that overturned the rule of the Bourbons, and that sent her enthusiastic volunteers singing the "Chant of the Rhone," or, as the ode is better known, the "Marseillaise Hymn," to protect the National Assembly and to secure the enforcement of the rights of the Constitution to France!

The old motto of the liberty-loving city was, *Sub cujas imperio summa libertas*, — "Liberty under any government."

Louis XIV., the "Grand Monarch" as he was called, on visiting Marseilles beheld the noble motto over the gate engraved in golden letters.

He scanned it with a jealous eye.

"Under previous kings that may have been possible," he said, "but not under me."

The motto was taken down, but its influence still lived in the minds of the people.

In the harbor of Marseilles one may see the flags of all the maritime nations of the world. It is the principal entrepôt of the Mediterranean, and one of the most safe, accessible, and sheltered of harbors. Twelve hundred vessels together may find accommodation at the quays; people of almost every race and language may be found there. Its water is somewhat discolored, but presents a beautiful panorama to the eye, with its city of ships and forests of masts. It was into this harbor that the bodies of the Mamelukes were thrown after the fall of Napoleon. The Mamelukes had been brought from Egypt by Napoleon, and had been given homes in Marseilles. They loved Napoleon, and when he fell they were seen to weep; when he seemed about to regain his lost power they were seen to rejoice, and were heard to say, *Napoleione, il è pion fort que tout*, — "Napoleon is stronger than all."

For this offence these poor children of Ishmael, who hoped for a protected life and quiet death on French soil, were murdered, and their bodies cast into the sea.

Marseilles entered into the Revolution of 1792 with a fiery zeal. It was her volunteers that gave the name of the "Marseillaise Hymn" to the most inspiring ode of liberty that music has ever produced. Here is the first stanza of it: —

> "Allons, enfans de la patrie !
> Le jour de gloire est arrivé.
> Contre nous de la tyrannie,
> L'étendard sanglant est levé,
> L'étendard sanglant est levé.
> Entendez-vous dans les campagnes
> Mugir ces féroces soldats ?
> Ils viennent, jusques dans vos bras,
> Egorger vos fils, vos compagnes !
> Aux armes, citoyens ! formez vos bataillons :
> Marchez ! marchons ! qu'un sang impur abreuve nos sillons !"

PUBLIC GARDEN (MARSEILLES)

Lamartine thus relates the origin of the song in his "History of the Girondists."

"Rouget de Lisle was born amid the mountains of Jura. He was a young officer at Strasburg. There he used to visit Dietrich, the mayor of Strasburg; and there, with Dietrich, his wife and daughters, indulged his taste for music. He was desired by Dietrich to write a hymn which should breathe the spirit of the Revolution. He wrote down the words and hastened to Dietrich. He found him in his garden digging up winter lettuces. It was so early in the morning that the old patriot's wife and daughters had not yet risen. Dietrich awoke them, sent for some of his friends like himself passionately fond of music, and capable of performing it. Rouget sang; Dietrich's eldest daughter accompanied him."

We will break in upon this narrative here to say, that it is commonly reported that the song was written in camp, in the night, and that the author fell asleep during a reverie which accompanied the inspiration of its composition. The last part of the stanza of the song in which are unexpected accidentals, is supposed to be the place where he became lost in his sleep, and the beginning of the chorus the place where he aroused from his slumber. This version of the story, however, may not be exactly true.

We continue the narrative of Lamartine : —

"At the first stanza all their countenances grew pale.
"At the second, tears flowed.
"At the last stanza the wildness of enthusiasm burst forth.
"Dietrich's wife and daughters, the old man himself, his friends, the young officer, threw themselves weeping into each other's arms.
"The hymn of the country was found!
"Dietrich, a few months later, walked to the scaffold to the sound of these very notes which had sprung forth at his hearth.
"The new song was performed at Strasburg. It flew from town to town, to all the popular orchestras. Marseilles adopted it, to be sung at the commencement and close of her clubs. The Marseillaise spread it through France, by singing it on their way to Paris. From this came the name of 'Marseillaise.'

"De Lisle himself became proscribed as a royalist, and shuddered as he heard his own song when flying along the pathway of the high Alps.

"'What do they call this hymn?' he asked of his guide.

"'The Marseillaise,' said the peasant.

"It was thus he learned the name of his own work.

"He escaped death with difficulty; the Revolution ran into madness, and no longer recognized the sound of its own voice."

> "Ye sons of France awake to glory!
> Hark! hark what myriads bid you rise!
> Your children, wives, and grandsires hoary,
> Behold their tears and hear their cries!
> Shall lawless tyrants, mischief breeding,
> With hireling hosts, a ruffian band,
> Affright and desolate the land,
> While truth and liberty lie bleeding?
>
> *Chorus.*
> To arms, to arms, ye brave!
> The avenging sword unsheathe;
> March on, march on, all hearts resolved
> On liberty or death!"

It became the war-song of France. It was one of the influences that overturned the throne. It was taken up by Jacobins, or Terrorists. The Girondists, who were the moderate republicans and embraced the wisest and best patriots of the nation, were overcome by the Terrorists, and twenty-one of their leaders were sentenced to the guillotine. They went forth from their prison to death, singing, —

> "Allons, enfans de la patrie!"

As one by one met his fate the song grew weaker, but it did not cease until the last head bowed to receive the fatal stroke.

Master Lewis, finding his health improved at Lisbon, had written to his substitute in the academy near Boston, to say that he would be willing to conduct a class of boys to Greece and take them over the course which their classical studies had suggested, — from Athens to Rome, following the historic track of Ulysses, Æneas, St. Paul, and of mythology, art, and Christianity.

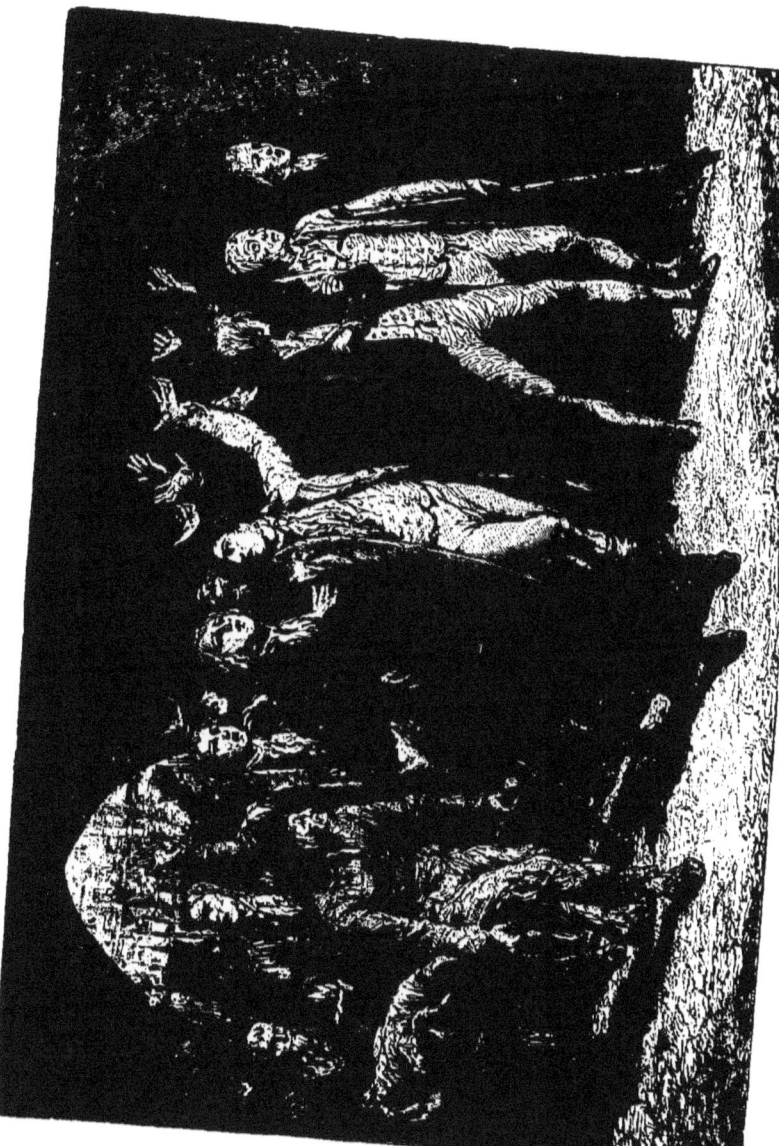

GIRONDINS SINGING THE MARSEILLES HYMN.

One of the teachers in the school, Mr. Beal, and three boys — Charlie Leland, William Clifton, and Herman Reed — formed a party to meet Master Lewis at Marseilles about the middle of June, whence it was arranged that the travellers — whom we will still call the

CHATEAU OF THE POPES, AVIGNON.

Class — should go to Genoa, Milan, and Venice, cross to Triest, and take the steamer for Athens, and from that city visit the shores of the Ægean and ascend Mt. Parnassus; then travel from Greece by the way of the island of Sicily and the city of Naples to Rome, ending the journey at Florence.

The Class remained two weeks at Marseilles. Here the boys applied themselves to study, visited often the lovely Public Garden, and made a trip along the River Rhone as far as Lyons, stopping at

CATHEDRAL OF LYONS.

Avignon to see the Château of the Popes, in which the Roman tribune Rienzi was once confined as a prisoner for dreaming the dream of Dante and trying to carry it into effect, — the unity of Italy.

PARK OF THE TETE D'OR (LYONS).

The Pope of Rome purchased this section of France in the Middle Ages, and governed it by a vice-legate, and several of the popes and anti-popes resided here. Here Petrarch spent his early years. He was a poet of humble birth, but his talents made him a companion of emperors, doges, and even popes. He was crowned at Rome amid splendid ceremonies. He met Laura, whose beauty he celebrates in

FOUNTAIN IN THE PARK OF LA TETE D'OR.

verse, at Avignon. He became greatly enamoured of her, for which we are sorry, because she was another man's wife, and there were many unappreciated maidens in the world at that time to whom it would have been more gallant for him to have given his attentions.

Lyons, the second city in population in France, presents the appearance of an immense manufactory. It is here that the most beautiful silks of the world are made. The city contains a fine cathedral, fifty squares, and a charming park or promenade, called the Park of the Tête D'Or.

The Class visited the heights of Fourvières, where Cæsar and his army once encamped. The ancient Gauls were heroes, and used to claim that they feared nothing but the fall of the sky. But Cæsar,

CHRISTIANITY ESTABLISHED IN GAUL.

who conquered three hundred nations, was too powerful for them, and Lyons became a province of Rome.

When Christianity went out from Rome on its missionary journeys over the world, it found a ready acceptance in Lyons, which became a centre for missionary work in Gaul. The Christians of Lyons became the victims of many persecutions, one of the most dreadful of which was under the reign of Septimius Severus.

The Class visited a church near the heights of Fourvières, the history of which filled them with wonder.

MOUNTED GAULS.

"This is a memorial church for martyrs," said Master Lewis. "It is called the Church of St. Irenæus. It is erected over the spot where the early Christians once met to pray; at their devotions they were attacked and massacred."

"How many were there?" asked Wyllys.

"History says there were twenty thousand."

"I never knew that the world ever witnessed such a tragic prayer-meeting as that," said Wyllys, walking to the church with a reverential feeling. "It seems impossible that such an event could have happened."

GAULS SUBJUGATED BY THE ROMANS.

"It was a terrible sacrifice. But Christianity lived. The Lyons missionaries preached through Gaul, and the heathen temples became changed to temples of Christ."

"The bodies of the Christians who were massacred at their devotions," continued Master Lewis, "were buried here, and many of them under this church."

Marseilles recalls the memory of one of the most terrible events during the present century, — the plague that visited that city in 1820, and destroyed nearly one third of the inhabitants.

It was brought to the city in a ship from the East. The people attempted to flee when its ravages became alarming, but a sanitary line was drawn around the city which it was death to pass.

The crisis was met with a spirit of Christian heroism by the clergy of the city, under the direction of the Bishop of Marseilles, Monseigneur de Belsunce. He penetrated into dens filled with dead and dying; he carried water to the sick; he rode through the streets administering comfort to those upon whom the plague had set its fatal mark; he even rode on the trumble that carried away the dead. Not only this, he rode on the dead cart with one of the worst of criminals for a driver. He literally followed the precepts of Christ.

One June evening, when Master Lewis and the boys were chatting in a parlor of the Grand Hotel, a valet-de-place came into the room and said to Master Lewis, —

"There is a lad in the office who is inquiring for you. Shall I take him to your room?"

Master Lewis said "No," but went into the hall after the valet-de-place.

"Who can it be?" said Wyllys to Tommy, as the two boys found themselves alone. "It seems strange that a lad should call and inquire for Master Lewis here."

"It may be some one from Boston," said Tommy. "It is too soon for any of the scholars to arrive; besides, the boys of the school who are to meet us are to come together in company with Mr. Beal."

Master Lewis was gone a long time, and returned at last alone.

"Who called?" asked Tommy.

"An old friend," said Master Lewis.

"A *lad?*"

"A boy I knew in America."

"An American boy! why did you not bring him in and introduce him to us?"

"He has taken a room in the hotel. He will be here presently."

BELZUNCE AMIDST THE PLAGUE-STRICKEN.

"What is his name?"

"Howe."

"Not George Howe?"

"Yes."

"How did he come here? He said that he hadn't the means to make the trip."

"In very much the same way as he made the zigzag journey before. He has a brother-in-law who is captain of one of the merchant steamers from New York to Liverpool. He came on the steamer with him to Liverpool, and paid his way by work in his friend's office. He travelled to London third-class; from London here by the way of Paris, at the cheapest fares; he obtained the one-hundred-dollar prize for scholarship in April; he proposes to go with us to Athens, and to leave us at Messena; he will meet there his brother-in-law's boat, which will there load with fruit for the New York market, and in that way he will return home."

"That is what I call pluck," said Tommy.

George presently appeared and received the warmest possible greeting.

"I cannot afford to remain here," he said, when the greetings were over. "I have only engaged a room here for one night."

"But you will stay here on my invitation several nights," said Wyllys, who was as generous as he was intelligent.

At Marseilles Master Lewis related to the boys an historic story associated with the city and the places they had visited on the Rhone.

THE CRUSADE OF THE CHILDREN.

"About the year 1212, there dwelt in an old province on the river Loire a shepherd's boy, named Stephen. He possessed an active imagination, and delighted in the tales of the palmers and the songs of the troubadours. He had a restless disposition, and aspired to see foreign lands.

"About one hundred years before his birth, the Christian princes of Europe had captured Jerusalem. The crusade that ended in this conquest had raised the victors to the very summit of fame. In palace and cottage, stories were told of the midnight march of the palmers from Emmaus to the hills over-looking the Holy City, and how their hearts burned within them by the way; how the sudden morning lighted up the brow of Olivet, and Jerusalem lay before them, pinnacled in the rising sun; how the great army fell prostrate at the sight, and kissed the earth; how Godfrey and Baldwin, and Robert and Raimond, shattered the army of the infidels, and scaled the sacred walls, and broke through the sacred gates; how, on that day of glory, Urban filled the papal throne, while Henry reigned in Germany, Philip in France, Rufus in England, and 'over all reigned the Lord Jesus Christ, to whom be honor, thanksgiving, and praise forever.'

"About the time of the birth of Stephen, Richard the Lion-Hearted returned from Palestine to England. His romantic exploits were then, and for many years afterwards, the favorite theme of every Catholic land. It was told how he had captured the island of Cyprus; how he was married there in flower-time; how he had fought with noble Saladin at Acre and Jaffa; how he had refused to look upon Jerusalem, as it lay beneath him gleaming in the sun, saying that he would not behold a city that he was unable to conquer.

"Stephen had been told these stories, and he dreamed of them by day and by night among the flocks on his own native hills. He longed for the time when his boyhood should pass away, and he would be able to join the palmers in some new crusade.

"In the year 1187 the Sultan Saladin conquered the city of Jerusalem. It was held by the infidels for many years, during which Europe frequently was agitated by plans and preparations for new crusades.

"One night the boy Stephen dreamed a remarkable dream. There came to him a pilgrim with a sorrowful face, and with garments tattered and torn. Stephen's heart was touched with pity at the sight, and he asked the stranger what he should do to relieve his distress.

"'Thou must preach a crusade to the young. Providence has allotted that the children shall recover the sepulchre of the Lord.'

"The boy Stephen afterwards said that he thought the pilgrim was the Saviour. He awoke, his soul filled with joy.

"He dreamed again, a day-dream. He fancied that he had unrolled the banner of the cross, and had gathered to his standard the children of every Christian land; that he went marching at their head, over the sunny provinces of France down to the gates of the sea; that a great fleet, waving its banners and gonfalons, bore them away; that they encamped on the moonlit plains of

PREACHING THE CRUSADE.

Syria among the roses; that they scaled the walls of Jerusalem, and sang anthems of thanksgiving at the Saviour's tomb.

"Stephen told his boy-companions his dream, and asked them if they were willing to take the cross as the emblem of their mission, and to go with him and fight beyond the sea. Elated beyond measure at the thought of engaging in so wonderful an enterprise, they promised to follow him whithersoever he should lead.

"The infatuated lad then left his flocks, and at once commenced to preach a crusade to the children. He announced himself as a prophet commissioned by Heaven to recover the Holy Sepulchre.

"What was more remarkable than his absurd dreaming, the children flocked around him wherever he went, and he pictured his mission and the glory that would attend it with such eloquence and power that he drew after him all who listened to his voice.

"He was followed at first by a small band of little ones, who prayed continually, 'Lord Jesus, restore thy cross to us!'

"The number increased to hundreds, then to thousands, then, when a multitude of boy-preachers had carried the delusion into the old cities of France, to tens of thousands.

"When Isabella, queen-dowager of England, was returning at this time to her home in Angoulême, in France, she found gatherings of children at the doors of the principal churches along the way. When she asked these children the cause of their assembling, they answered, with downcast looks, 'Solyma lies in ruins.'

"The delusion exerted so powerful an influence on the youth of France, that a great number of parents were unable to control their children. 'No bolts, no bars,' says a historian of the young enthusiasts, ' no fear of fathers, no love of mothers, could hold them back.' Girls, as well as boys, ran away from their homes, and swelled the procession that followed Stephen. Whole villages were depopulated of children.

"'Solyma lies in ruins!'

"The cry of the children filled all Southern France.

"Both the Church and the Government of France were divided in opinion in respect to this remarkable movement. The more intelligent prelates discountenanced the young enthusiasts, while the laity held that God, through the agency of 'babes and sucklings,' was about to display His power in a signal manner on earth.

"The king, Philip Augustus, a man of prudence and sagacity, being uncertain as to what course he ought to pursue, called for the opinions of the master of the high school at Paris. This learned man was convinced that Stephen was nothing but a dreamy, imaginative boy, and that the whole movement was a delusion. Philip, therefore, ordered the young enthusiasts to return to their homes. But only a part of the boys obeyed the royal order.

"Stephen pretended to work miracles, and people regarded him as inspired, and believed his words to be a higher authority than the king's. So fully were they given over to his influence that they held the very threads of his garments as sacred.

"This hero-worship excited the young prophet's vanity. He rode in a chariot decorated with flags, and attended by a numerous guard. The boy-preachers told their followers that, when they should reach the coast, the sea would retire, and they would be able to pass over to Palestine dry shod. With this expectation they marched at last towards the Mediterranean, and came to Marseilles.

"They saw the splendors of the city and the beauty of the sea. Still was their watchword, as they thought of the desolation of Jerusalem, —

"'Solyma lies in ruins!'

"But the Mediterranean did not retire before them. The great harbor of Marseilles was covered with vessels, and the leaders of the expedition began to look about for seamen to take the youthful army across the sea. They found ship-owners, at last, who professed to be very pious, and who agreed to take them, free of charge, to Syria.

"The ships were soon ready, and one by one they left behind the bright spires and dark towers of the old commercial city.

"The weather was fair, the wind favorable, and the hearts of the boys delighted alike in the novelty of the enterprise and in the beauty of the sky, the air, and the sea.

"One day the sky was overcast. The wind arose. The vessels were crowded, and when night settled upon the deep the boys began to be afraid. The wind increased in power until it became a gale, and a part of the fleet was driven on the rocks near Sardinia, and went down, and all on board perished.

"The remaining vessels directed their course not to Syria but to Egypt. Here the young crusaders discovered that they had been betrayed into the hands of slave-traders, and that the ship-owners were bad men who had deceived them, by the appearance of piety, to sell them as slaves. They all were sold to the Egyptians and Persians, the greater part of them to the people of Alexandria. Four hundred monks were bought by the caliph of Bagdad, and nearly a thousand boys by the governor of Alexandria."

CRUSADERS ON THE WAY TO PALESTINE.

Tommy Toby made the acquaintance of several lively French boys while the party tarried at Marseilles. These boys entertained very singular ideas about America and Americans. They believed all Americans to be immensely rich, — like the old incas, to whose stores of gold there was hardly a limit.

One of these boys was named Pierre Cambronne, of excellent family at Nantes, who were now stopping at Marseilles at the Grand Hotel. He had a younger brother named Jacques, who was studying German with an old pedagogue from Strasburg.

Tommy was attracted to Pierre by a wonderful feat which the latter performed one evening at the hotel. He was passing the Cambronnes' room, the door being open, when he heard a merry laugh,

PIERRE.

and to his great astonishment saw Pierre lying on his stomach on the floor and making of his body an almost perfect wheel. There was a fork attached to the lad's heel, and with this he was able to convey pieces of fruit to his mouth.

Tommy at once determined to know, if possible, this wonderful boy.
Soon after he caught Jacques in the act of drawing a grotesque effigy
of the old German schoolmaster on the wall of a corridor leading to the recitation room. Tommy laughed; Jacques colored; the old teacher's step was heard approaching, when Tommy helped Jacques to rub out the picture, after which the two boys recognized each other, and Jacques introduced Tommy to his brother Pierre, who was such a skilful gymnast.

JACQUES.

"You are an American," said Pierre, "and have money to travel all over the world."

"I am from Maine," said Tommy.

"Maine" had an aristocratic sound to the French brothers.

"I am studying near Boston," continued Tommy, "and am travelling with my teacher."

"Is the Province of Maine in Boston?" asked Pierre. "Has it gold mines, diamond mines, monkeys?" he added, showing what a vivid and brilliant picture the name of Maine had brought to the boy's fancy.

"No," said Tommy, glancing at Master Lewis who was near, and laughing.

"Tell them the truth," said Master Lewis in English. "Maine is chiefly woods, you know," he added, as he saw that Tommy was unwilling to spoil the splendid fancies of his French friends.

"How do the young gentlemen amuse themselves in Maine?" asked Pierre.

"They go logging in winter and fishing in summer," said Master Lewis to Tommy, in English. "When they get old enough they go to Boston and become clerks."

"They sail on the Penobscot and the Kennebec," said Tommy in French. "Then they become merchants."

These American names sounded like titles of renown to the French boys. They seemed to regard Tommy as an heir to estates of unbounded magnificence.

In the summer evenings the people of Marseilles seek recreation in the multitudinous pleasure-boats of the cool and beautiful harbor. Tommy was several times invited by these French boys to sail with them. The little boat they used would skim along in the moonlight among the great city of ships, and Tommy inadvertently surprised his new friends by telling them that he had never enjoyed anything so much even in Maine.

"How many ships enter the harbor in a year?" asked Tommy in one of these delightful summer-evening excursions.

"More than ten thousand," said Pierre.

Ships now and then arrived in the harbor from South-American ports containing parrots and monkeys, and these had probably suggested to the French boys their peculiar views of Maine.

There was a famous South-American parrot near the hotel, which was a wonder. Its great delight was to interrupt an earnest talker with the words, —

"You are a liar and a villain!"

Trades-people who called at the café where it was kept, and were loud-mouthed in extolling their wares, were certain to be checked by the startling and often true declaration, —

"You are a liar and a villain!"

One day Tommy went to see the bird with Master Lewis. The parrot was quite silent. At last Tommy began to tell Master Lewis about some new kindness Pierre and Jacques had shown him, when the bird slowly bent down his head in a very scrutinizing way, and said:

"You are a liar and a villain!"

"Perhaps he refers to what you told your French friends about the State of Maine," said Master Lewis.

"I told them the truth," said Tommy.

"YOU ARE A LIAR AND A VILLAIN!"

"No one tells the truth who makes a false impression wilfully," said Master Lewis. "I hope you will enlighten your friends as to what the State of Maine is, and what is your true position in society."

Tommy promised that he would. We hope he did. He liked to exaggerate a story, and Master Lewis was determined to check this tendency to untruth. So, when he found him using free fancy after this little episode had happened, he used to say to him quietly, —

"Remember the parrot of Marseilles!"

CHAPTER VIII.

GENOA, MILAN, AND VENICE.

GENOA. — MILAN CATHEDRAL. — THE VENETIAN REPUBLIC. — STORY OF THE DWARF OF LOMBARDY.

FOR several days about the middle of June the Class impatiently awaited the arrival of the second party of the Zigzag Club. The boys, except George, had been nearly two weeks in Marseilles, and were anxious to start on the Eastern trip. Mr. Beal, with the three expected lads, arrived about the 14th. The Class now consisted of Master Lewis, Mr. Beal, Wyllys Wynn, Tommy Toby, George Howe, Charles Leland, William Clifton, and Herman Reed. As Master Lewis desired to spend the last eight days of June in Greece, the party immediately took a steamer for Genoa.

In the purple and vermilion of a June afternoon the Class sighted the shores of Italy, and saw Genoa — *Genoa la Superba* — lifting her hundred sun-crowned domes and spires above the blue sea. As the boat drew near the coast the city seemed set on fire by the sunset and to blaze against the sky. Then slowly the splendor faded, and with it, alas! the brightest vision that the Class had of Genoa dissolved.

The Class took lodgings in an inn that had been a palace. The next morning they rode through the town. The streets were narrow, full of bad smells, and thronged with idlers and beggars. Massive buildings everywhere appeared, recalling the palmy days when the city filled the Mediterranean with her ships and enriched her palaces with the treasures of the East. The donkeys seemed to be the servants of the Genoese in most kinds of hard work; they were to be seen almost everywhere, most of them having a much-abused look.

DONKEYS.

Here and there were groups of gossipers, and in these the dark figure of a fat, good-humored looking priest several times appeared.

The Class visited the Cathedral, or the Duomo as it is called, — a pile of antique magnificence which seemed to be slowly fading, like the pictures that adorn its walls. It is said to have been a Jewish Synagogue before the Saviour was born. Its chief attraction is the Chapel of John the Baptist.

The Class was told by the guide that this place was regarded as particularly holy; women were allowed to enter it only once a year, because it was the dancing of a woman which caused John to be beheaded.

In the Chapel is a marble chest, in which is said to be the remains of St. John.

"But the head of St. John is at Amiens, France," said Tommy Toby. "The shrine containing it was shown to us last year."

The guide shook his head, and said, —

"These are the true relics of St. John; Genoa has the true relics."

GENOESE.

The church contains another curious and greatly-esteemed relic, — a glass dish, once supposed to be a solid emerald, which the Queen of Sheba is said to have given to Solomon, and which is believed to have been used at the Last Supper. There is another story associated with it which it seems wanting in reverence to relate, and so we pass it by in silence.

The Class remained two days at Genoa, then took the cars for Milan. The ride was delightful through a land of marvellous beauty, past mountain slopes rich with gardens, and peaks crowned with the pure gold of sunshine.

All along the route were tunnels, dark but cool. It was out of the shadow into the sun, out of the gloomy recesses into the heart of the hills, into paradises of balmy air, verdure, and bloom. Some of the tunnels were so long that it took nearly a quarter of an hour to pass through them, and when the passage was made, the light of the clear Italian air and sky seemed bewildering.

A forest of spires began to be seen in the mellow air, like the masts of a distant port. It was an inspiring sight, and the Class looked for it again and again as the train wound along. It was its first view of that wonder of the world, the Cathedral of Milan.

Milan is second in splendor among the cities of Italy. Its history is older than the Christian era; it was the seat of the old Court of Lombardy, and under the first Napoleon was made the capital of the Cis-Alpine Republic and of the Kingdom of Italy. In the Middle Ages it was famous for its manufacture of armor and dress; hence the word *millner*.

It would require a volume to describe the Cathedral of Milan; it has more than seven thousand statues, and it would consume seven thousand pages to describe them, which would be more than our friends might like to read. It is to have three thousand more statues; so, were we to attempt a description of them, our story would be incomplete. It has fifteen hundred bas-reliefs, and more are to be added. It has been centuries in building, and has cost more than one hundred millions of dollars; it will require centuries to complete it, and untold millions will doubtless be spent upon it unless the growth of Republicanism in Italy shall prevent the completion of the marvellous plan. It is a mountain of beauty; in sunlight a glory, in moonlight a charm; a marble colossus, a bewilderment of art. The most glowing dreams of Raphael, Michael Angelo, and Canova all turn into marble and fresco and gems and canvas here.

Go up the one hundred and eighty-two marble steps and stand in the highest spire. Old Lombardy with its thrilling traditions lies before you, glowing in the sunlight under the shadows of the Alps. The statues of multitudinous saints, pinnacled in air, are beneath you; the very beams are carved with flowers; fifteen hundred kinds of plants are represented in the limitless tracery.

Descend, and enter. The majestic windows burn with pictures, and one beholds the Scriptures as in a vision. Angels seem floating in the air, and apostles and prophets appear to have descended with new benedictions upon the world.

"This must be the world's masterpiece," said Wyllys Wynn. "I could never have imagined anything so grand. It is a miracle."

"Of work," said Master Lewis.

From Milan the Class proceeded to Venice by rail.

"When we arrive at Venice," said Tommy, "shall we be taken to our hotel by a carriage or a gondola?"

"By a gondola," said Master Lewis.

"And enter the city in fine style," continued Tommy, "the gondola trailing along the waters its cloth of purple and gold."

"What gave you such an idea as that?" asked Master Lewis.

"Some picture I have seen," replied Tommy.

As the city of the sea drew near, a thousand lights were seen dancing in mid air and dropping their fires into the sea. The whole distance seemed like night in fairyland.

A long dark object, looking like a hearse, received the Class at the station, and glided away under the direction of two as dark-looking men.

"Is this a gondola?" asked Tommy. "I thought a gondola was canopied with silk, and carved in antique figures, and gilded with gold."

"The men who are propelling the old scow do not look as though they own any extra velvet to trail along the sea," said George Howe.

The mysterious boat passed under bridges, and past dark melancholy houses rising from the water, and reached at last the Grand Canal, which enchanted the Class like a vision of beauty. The Venice of romance was before them. Palaces seemed to lift their glimmering walls almost to the stars. Gondolas with colored lights were shooting hither and thither; music was heard, recalling the old tales of the songs of the gondoliers. All was mazy, strange, bewildering.

The Class were taken to the Hotel d'Europe.

The first visit that the Class made in Venice was to the Ducal Palace, famed in history, romance, song, and in paintings and pictures innumerable. Like the Louvre, it was a palace of pictures. Here were to be seen the largest picture in the world and the finest productions of most of the world's great masters in Venetian art. The Grand Hall or Senate Chamber was adorned with portraits of the seventy-two doges of Venice, — grim, venerable-looking men, who saw the republic rise, reach her meridian splendor, and decline, during a period of more than a thousand years.

There was among these portraits a space covered with a black veil.

"What is the meaning of that?" asked Wyllys.

"Read the inscription," said Master Lewis. "It is in Latin."

Wyllys read, —

"HIC EST LOCUS MARINI FALERTO, DECAPITATI PRO CRIMINIBUS."

"Who was Marini Falerto?" asked Wyllys.

"He was the Marino Falieri of tragic dramas and romances," said Master Lewis. "He was a traitor. He endeavored to destroy the republic of Venice and to make himself a king."

"I never felt before what a dismal thing it must be to be a traitor, and to remain so in the memory of the world forever."

At the head of a flight of steps, called the "Giant's Staircase," was shown the place where Marino Faliero, or Falieri, was beheaded.

"Venice must have been a model republic," said Tommy, — "only one traitor among the doges in more than a thousand years! George

ON THE CANAL.

is always extolling American institutions. Our republic is only about a hundred years old. Republics seem hardly to be anything new under the sun, after all."

"What kind of a republic was Venice?" asked George of Tommy.

"I don't know; it was just a republic."

Presently the Class were shown two small holes in a stone wall.

"The Lion's Mouth was there," said the guide.

"What lion's mouth?" asked Tommy.

"Have n't you read? When one wished to accuse another in the times of the doges, he wrote a note and put it into the Lion's Mouth."

"And then?" asked Tommy.

"It was examined by the Council of Three."

"And then?"

"They condemned the man to death, and the secret police arrested him, and he was led over the Bridge of Sighs, and was never heard of again."

"What became of him?"

"Sometimes he was put into a dungeon without light or air, and there he was left to die. Sometimes he was sewed up in a sack and drowned. Then they had a dreadful machine for taking off the heads of certain victims. No one who went over the Bridge of Sighs ever returned again."

"Could not the victim appeal?" asked Tommy.

"Appeal! What was there to appeal to? His own family did not so much as know of his arrest. There were a thousand or more patricians who governed the republic. From these the senate was chosen; this senate chose a council of ten, and this council chose a council of three; and these used to hold night sessions, masked and robed in scarlet, and they condemned to death whom they liked."

"That was a modern republic indeed!" said George. "What were a poor man's liberties worth under such a rule as that? Even you, Tommy, will confess our republic is an improvement on such a system."

"Was it always so in Venice?" asked Tommy.

"At the beginning of the republic I believe the doge and senate

VENETIAN WATER-CARRIER.

were elected by the people. The people surrendered their rights to the aristocracy. The government then became the rule of the privileged classes, and grew tyrannical."

Venice is a fascinating city. The common people are simple in their taste, dress, and habits, and their appearance contrasts strongly with the fading splendors of the structures of the period when

"Venice sat in state, throned on her hundred isles."

The Class spent a morning at the Square of St. Mark, which Napoleon said was the most beautiful spot in the world, and visited the Cathedral of St. Mark, where the remains of St. Mark are supposed to rest.

We will close this chapter with a curious story which Master Lewis related to the Class on the journey to Milan.

THE DWARF OF LOMBARDY.

Sometime during the early part of the sixth century there was born in a small village, near the grand old city of Verona, a very remarkable dwarf. His name was Bertholde. At the age of manhood his deformities were very marked. His stature was short; his head was of enormous size; his ears nearly covered the sides of his head; his under lip hung down on his chin, and from his mouth projected two large teeth.

Nature often compensates the unfortunate by endowing them with remarkable faculties, hiding behind a rough exterior her rarest intellectual gems.

Bertholde possessed a wonderful mind. Everything seemed clear to him. In point of intellect he was as superior to others as he was inferior to them in form.

Alboin, the founder of the Kingdom of Lombardy, held his court, at this time, at Verona. Attracted to the royal residence by the fame of its splendors, Bertholde determined to have an interview with the king. In those palmy days no guards frowned at the palace gates, and having resolved to see his sovereign he entered the palace and walked boldly into the royal apartment.

With the air of a philosopher he approached the king, and, without removing his hat, took a seat at his side. The king neither knew what to make of the creature himself, nor of his singular behavior; and the courtiers were struck with wonder.

"Who are you?" exclaimed the king. "How did you come into the world? From what country do you come?"

THE DWARF OF LOMBARDY.

"I am a man," answered the dwarf deliberately. "I came into the world in the manner that Providence sent me, and my country is the world."

Pleased with the answer and with the dwarf's philosophical manner and cast of mind, the good king asked a number of curious questions.

"What is that which has the swiftest wings?" asked the monarch.

"Thought," answered the dwarf.

"What is that gulf that is never full?"

"The avarice of a miser."

"What is most disagreeable in the character of the young?"

"Self-conceit."

"What is the most ridiculous in the old?"

"Love."

"Who caress us the most?"

"Those who deceive us, and those who intend to do so."

The kind-hearted king was so much entertained by the good sense of the dwarf that at the close of the interview he promised to give him anything he desired, as a mark of his good-will.

"I desire what I defy you to give."

"What?"

"Happiness, which kings are unable to impart, for they have less of it than others."

"You would not be a courtier?" asked the king, alluding to his plain, simple manners.

"No; unhappy as is my lot, I would not be a slave; moreover, I am neither a knave nor a liar, and consequently I have not the qualities for that fine employment."

"What, then, do you seek at my court?"

"What I have been unable to find, for I had imagined that sovereigns were as much above other men as steeples are above common houses, but I soon found that I had esteemed them too highly."

The king, thinking that the ready wit of the dwarf might be of service to him, gave him permission to reside at court. Bertholde accordingly became a very conspicuous character at Verona, and was finally appointed Prime Minister of Lombardy.

Bertholde, like many statesmen in the world's history who have dared to deal sincerely with their superiors, at one time fell under the displeasure of the court, and was condemned to be hanged.

"I have one request to ask," he said to the king.

"Name it."

"That I may choose the tree on which I am willing to die."

"You shall have your request."

Bertholde with two executioners went into the forest to find the tree. He trudged along, and found many fine trees with long arms, but none of them met the requirement. The two executioners became weary with travelling, and sat down to rest, and Bertholde returned to the court.

"Why have you come back?" he was asked.

"I could not find the tree."

So the king spared his life.

The Class crossed the Gulf to Trieste, and there took one of the fine Austrian Lloyd's steamers for Athens.

CHAPTER IX.

PARNASSUS.

THE APPROACH TO ATHENS. — THE ACROPOLIS. — MT. PENTELICUS. — TOMMY'S STORY OF
THE HEROIC AGE. — A SABBATH ON MARS' HILL. — THE JOURNEY TO PARNASSUS. —
PARNASSUS.

AM sitting on the deck of a steamer from Sicily; the screw of the steamer churns the green waters into foam; the pure sky is flushed with purple, and in the distance precipices dotted with verdure are lifting their heads above the sun-flooded sea.

"'That is Greece!'

"So says Master Lewis, and visions of what I have been reading pass through my mind.

"'We left behind us in America,' says Master Lewis, 'cities that are two hundred years old. We shall soon be brought in view of cities and towns that have a history two thousand years older than the Christian era, and about which gather the traditions and poetry of nearly four thousand years. Think of the keels that have crossed the waters into which we are passing, — for we are approaching the peninsula of Sparta, — the Phœnician ships in the days that are hardly remembered; the Persian fleets from the north; the Egyptian vessels from the south, and the Roman galleys from the west; great war-ships of the eagles, the crescent, and the cross. Homer, the Cæsars, blind Dandolo of Venice, and that great light of the Gentile world the Apostle Paul, all passed over the track we are passing, and looked upon the cliffs on which we are looking; and in those long past centuries the sea and the sky were the same as we see them now.'

"The bells are striking. The steamer slackens her speed. Small boats are moving towards her.

"Before us is Piræus, the port of Athens, four miles from the city, and the boats are coming to take us to the custom house.

"An officer on the ship has been speaking to Master Lewis, and pointing towards the west. Master Lewis turns to the Class, and says, —

"'That is the hill on which Xerxes sat more than two thousand years ago, and from which he watched the battle of Salamis. His throne was gold, standing on silver feet. He was arrayed in splendid robes, and around him were gathered his courtiers with tablets in their hands to record the heroic deeds of the expected battle, to be engraved on the halls of Babylon. He looked down on the one hand on the largest army ever seen in the world, and on the other hand upon a fleet of more than a thousand ships. Herodotus claims that his army numbered millions.

"'In the waters that lie before you his great fleet was defeated; the sea itself seemed to fight for the little fleet of the Greeks, and Xerxes fled from his overturned throne at the sight of the wrecks of his navy that filled the straits, and of the bodies of Persian warriors drifting on the tide. He escaped from Greece in a single barque, going back to the palace of his queen, the beautiful Esther of the Bible.'

"All now is hurry on the steamer. I will close this entry in my journal with one oft-quoted verse, —

"'A king sat on the rocky brow
   Which o'erlooks sea-born Salamis,
And ships by thousands lay below,
   And men in nations, — all were his!
He counted them at break of day,
   And when the sun set, where were they?'"

Such was a part of an entry in Wyllys Wynn's journal on the 23d of June 18—.

The Piræus, or port of Athens, was not an interesting looking spot. There was a sort of casino or restaurant near by, where the descendants of the noble Greeks were seen playing cards, drinking wine, and smoking tobacco.

"I do not see much to remind me of Demosthenes, Socrates, and Plato *here*," said Tommy Toby.

Hackmen were talking vigorous Greek to Master Lewis.

"What a looking hack!" said Tommy, as the carriage he was to take was pointed out to him. "I thought I was going to ride into Athens behind two of those horses you read about, and in a *chariot*. Never mind, — let me ride outside."

The road to Athens lies between the ruins of the famous walls of Themistocles. The first wonderful sight on approaching the city is the Acropolis on the rocky hill, where the old temples of Attica once stood in unsurpassed beauty, and where their ruins still stand in picturesque desolation. This citadel, or fortress, with its temples was the pride of ancient Greece, was deemed the perfection and model of all classic art, and was the wonder and envy of the world. Its chief temple, the Parthenon, was regarded as the finest structure in history, and its site as the most beautiful in the world.

The Class took rooms in the Hotel d'Angleterre. The windows looked out upon an enclosed garden where the birds sang delightfully in the morning, and towards the mountain range of Hymettus where the bees made honey in the time of Plato, and over which the sun rose clear, morning after morning, in a resplendent sky.

The Acropolis, though in ruins, is still the pride of Athens, and the grandest monument in Greece. The word *acropolis*, as applied to Greek cities, means the high point of the town, or a citadel. Athens is walled in by mountains, and a hill rising one hundred and fifty feet direct from the plain on which the city is built furnished a natural platform for her citadel. There were acropolises at Argos, Thebes,

THE PROPYLÆA

and Corinth, but none of them were so beautiful in situation and in the grandeur of their temples as Athens.

The Parthenon was the glory of the Acropolis. It was built in

VIEW OF ATHENS FROM THE ACROPOLIS.

the golden age of Pericles and Phidias, in the palmy years of peace that followed the Persian wars. It is supposed to have cost one thousand talents (£700,000.) It is a structure of pure marble; even the tiles on its roof were Parian marble. It was dedicated to Minerva, and was filled with the sculptures of Phidias, the greatest master of Greek art. It contained a statue of the goddess, which with the exception of the statue of Jupiter at Olympia, also by Phidias, was the most celebrated in the world.

The statue was of ivory and gold.

It was Pericles' misfortune to have bitter political enemies, for he was an ardent republican, and held to the equal rights of all men in affairs of state. His enemies sought to injure him by attacking his friends.

They accused Phidias of having taken for his own use some of the gold appropriated for the statue of Minerva.

Phidias caused the statue to be dismantled and the gold to be weighed, and so triumphantly established his innocence.

He was then accused of impiety for having engraved his own likeness and that of Pericles on the shield of the goddess. This charge was true, and he was thereupon cast into prison, where he died of sickness or of poison.

The Class made its first visit to the Acropolis early in the morning, passing through the ruins of the Propylæa, a temple that once formed the resplendent portals to the citadel. It was built in the age of Pericles, when it was reached by a flight of sixty steps.

The sun had just risen, filling all the clear sky with splendor. It was such a sunrise as the boys had never seen before. There was no vapor in the sky, no contrast of light and shade, sunbeam and cloud, nothing but infinite clearness and calm; just as the Greek poets described it thousands of years ago.

"I do not wonder," said Wyllys, "that the people here thought that the sun was indeed a god."

The outlook was most glorious. A purple tint hung over the far-off mountains; Mt. Hymettus was a flood of gold; Salamis was in full view, also the calm waters of the Mediterranean. Below the Acropolis was the beautiful temple of Theseus, and at no long distance the

TEMPLE OF THE WINGLESS VICTORY.

ruins of the temple of Jupiter Olympus. On the south-eastern slope of the Acropolis was the majestic ruin of the Odeum, or theatre of Herod Atticus, in which the works of the great Greek poets were once heard.

After breakfast on the same day, the Class took horses and rode to

THEATRE OF HEROD.

the summit of Mt. Pentelicus, some ten miles from Athens, to see the plain and battle-field of Marathon. The mountain is thirty-five hundred feet high. The scenery along the route was highly picturesque, and towards the top of the mountain the views became grand and imposing. From the top the Class looked down, not only on the plain of Marathon, but on the whole plan of Athens, the islands of Salamis, and the Ægean.

"The mountains look on Marathon —
And Marathon looks on the sea."

While here, Master Lewis, who sought to make every excursion as instructive as he was able, translated a description of the battle of Marathon from Herodotus, and explained the manner in which the great army of Darius was overthrown by Miltiades.

The Class galloped back to Athens in the tranquil light of a summer afternoon, admiring the beauty of the Acropolis as it came into view, standing out with a strange distinctness in the transparent air.

In the evening, at the hotel, Tommy Toby related the story of the heroic age of Greece, an exercise which he had been preparing by some quite heroic reading, and which he chose to call an account of

THE ZIGZAGS OF ULYSSES.

"The Golden Age had passed, and the Silver Age. Jupiter was king now, and his throne was on Mount Olympus, and it was the Heroic Age down in the world below."

"How high is Olympus?" asked Charlie Leland.

"Almost ten thousand feet high. You will see it in a few days."

"Did any one ever go up to see?"

"See what?"

THE COUNCIL OF THE GODS.

"Jupiter."

"When?"

"When he was there."

"I don't know. Olympus was an awful hard mountain to climb. Its top is all covered with snow most of the year, and with clouds much of the time. Jupiter had thunder-bolts in his hand that Vulcan made for him in his blacksmiths' shops, which were his volcanoes. Some of his volcanoes — smithies — have n't gone out yet. Ætna was one, — you may still see it; so what I tell you is just as true now as it ever was, and you must not ask any more questions.

"There was one person, certainly, who, according to the ancient stories, 'went up to see,' as Charlie expresses it. That was Ganymede."

"Who was Ganymede?" asked Charlie.

"He was a lad that tended sheep on Mount Ida. The gods wanted a cup-bearer up on Olympus. They had Vulcan first, but he hobbled; and then they had Hebe, but she tumbled down one day and broke all her dishes, and spilled the tea and coffee — no, nectar. Then the gods sent down a great eagle — Jupiter's eagle — to seize the shepherd boy Ganymede, and bring him up to their palaces. They made him cup-bearer, and he answered very well."

"Did he ever come back?"

"No. They gave him nectar or ambrosia, or some other kind of syrup to drink, and they made him immortal."

"Oh!"

"Well, I started to tell a story. It was, as I said, all very extraordinary times. Old Atlas was standing away out in the uninhabited regions of the twilight holding up the world on his back, and—"

"And what became of Atlas?" asked Charlie.

"There were some maiden ladies called the Gorgons, who lived in the regions beyond the sunset. One of these was named Medusa,—Miss Medusa Gorgon. Now any beau that went to see Miss Medusa, and looked into her face, was turned into a stone. There was a Greek hero named Perseus, who succeeded in a plan of cutting Miss Medusa's head off without looking into her face. He put the head in a bag and showed it to Atlas; and poor old Atlas after holding the world on his back for no one knows how many years was turned into a great stone mountain. You have heard of the Atlas Mountains?—well, *that* is *him*."

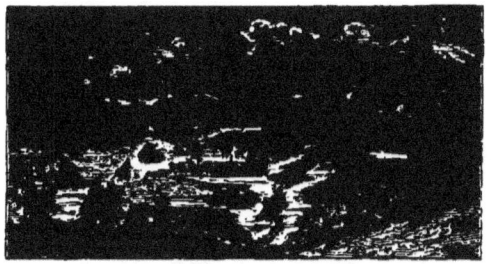

PLAIN OF TROY.

"Oh!"

"Well, there roamed a shepherd on Mt. Ida, a king's son, very handsome, whose name was Paris.

"Once, when the gods and goddesses were having a feast, the Goddess of Discord threw a golden apple into the merry assembly, and on it was inscribed,—

"'This is for the fairest.'

"Juno thought it was meant for her.

"Pallas thought it was meant for her.

"Venus thought it was meant for her.

"Then there was trouble, and hard words, and much truth-speaking; but they finally decided to submit the question as to which was the fairest to handsome Paris, the shepherd on Mt. Ida.

"Juno said if he would decide in her favor she would give him a throne.

"Pallas said if he would decide for her she would make him wise.

"Venus said if he would decide in her interest she would give him the handsomest woman in the world for a wife.

"Now Paris ought to have decided in favor of Pallas if the reward was to be considered, for he needed wisdom greatly enough, as you will presently see. But he decided in favor of Venus.

"Paris was a Trojan. Troy was, as Virgil says, 'an ancient city.' It was in Asia on the shores of the Ægean, and at this time old Priam was king. He lived snugly in a fine palace, with his wife Hecuba and a family of some nineteen children, of whom Paris was not the most promising.

HELEN AND PRIAM ON THE RAMPARTS.

"Paris went to visit the Greek kings. While he was in Greece he met a beautiful woman named Helen, the wife of Menelaus; and one day, when her husband was away, she eloped with handsome Paris, who brought her to Troy. She was, perhaps, the handsomest woman in all the world.

"When Menelaus came home and found what Paris had done, he called on all the Greek heroes to make war upon Troy and recover the faithless Helen.

"The war lasted ten years. You may read about it in Homer and Virgil,— the great deeds of Hector the son of Priam; the valor of brave Achilles; the death of Patroclus, and the lofty funeral pile on which his body was laid, and the wonderful funeral rites around his bier.

"In the war Paris, the cause of all the trouble, was at last killed. But the

Trojans would not give up Helen, for two other brothers of Paris and sons of poor old Priam had fallen in love with her.

"There was an image in Troy called the Palladium. The Greeks discovered that the gods had decreed that Troy should never be taken while the Palladiam remained within its walls. Ulysses, one of the Greek heroes, climbed over the walls of the city at night and stole the wonderful image.

"The Greeks now pretended to abandon the siege. They appeared to sail away, and the Trojans, overjoyed at the supposed event, came out of the city and rushed down to the shore.

"Here they were astonished at finding an immense wooden horse.

"A man came out of the rocks, Sinon by name —he certainly was a sinner by nature—and said he had been left behind by the Greeks, who had gone home, and that the wooden horse was a sacred image, and that if they were to take it into Troy it would be a new Palladium. Laocoön, a Trojan priest, did not believe the story, but declared Sinon to be a spy,—for which plain speaking there came two serpents out of the sea and destroyed him and his two sons.

FUNERAL PILE OF PATROCLUS.

"The simple Trojans took the gigantic horse into the city. The horse was full of Greeks like a great siege machine, and at night they left their hiding-place and set fire to the city. The Grecian fleet, that had been hiding behind the island of Tenedos, came up again; and so Troy was taken, Priam was killed, and Helen, who was not worth any hero's attention, was retaken. Ulysses killed one of the little sons of Priam, for which he was punished by the gods.

"How Ulysses was punished for his part in the destruction of Troy is told in the 'Odyssey.'

"He was returning to Ithaca with his fleet, when a great storm assailed him and drove his ships into a strange sea. He first came to the island of the lotus eaters — "

"About which you may read in Tennyson," said Master Lewis.

"He next came to a kind of ice-cream saloon in an enormous cavern, all

BLINDING OF THE CYCLOPS.

full of milk and cream and great cheeses. It was on a rocky island. He stopped to take some refreshments, and was having a feast fit for a king, and making merry with his companions, when a great flock of sheep came rushing into the cave. Behind them came a giant, tall as a tower, with only one eye, which was in the middle of his forehead. He had a tree for a staff. His name was Polyphemus, a workman of Vulcan, and one of the Cyclops, a race of giants.

"The Greeks were terribly frightened, especially when he dashed two of their number upon the floor of the cave and then eat them up. He put a great rock at the mouth of the cave, and fell asleep, evidently intending to eat up the others in the morning, or some other day.

"The next day the Greeks offered him wine. He drank so much that he fell into a deep sleep, and the Greeks put out his eye with his own staff, and so escaped. As they were sailing away, Polyphemus hurled great rocks after them: you may see the rocks there yet, as big as islands.

"Ulysses next came to the Island of Winds, and was supplied by Æolus with wind-bags enough to take him home. But his crew pricked the wind-bags, and that caused a great storm, which drove him back to the island again, and Æolus, as a punishment, would give him no more wind.

"He was tortured by the temptations of the Sirens, bumped about in the straits between Scylla and Charybdis, and finally was wrecked, and escaped on a raft which drifted upon the island of Scheria, whence the king sent him home to Ithaca after he had been absent twenty years.

ESCAPE OF ULYSSES.

"When Ulysses arrived in Ithaca, he found that his troubles were not yet ended. There were one hundred Ionian chiefs in his palace, all come to court Penelope his wife, or the supposed widow of Ulysses. She was placed in a very perplexing situation, and to put off her one hundred Ionian lovers she told them that she could not decide which she would marry until she had woven a winding-sheet for her father-in-law. She undid at night all that she wove by

ULYSSES RECOGNIZED BY EURYCLEIA.

day, and so no progress was made on the fabric. How Ulysses came to her in disguise, and was only recognized in his palace by his dog and an old servant, and how he slew Penelope's one hundred lovers, more or less, is all written in the 'Odyssey,' which is a far more entertaining book than any of the wonder stories now written for boys and girls; and referring you to that, I will bring my story to an end."

A SABBATH ON MARS' HILL.

The next day was the Sabbath.

"How shall we spend the day?" asked Wyllys Wynn of Master Lewis. "By going to the Greek church?"

"I have a plan," said Master Lewis. "If the Class will go out with me after breakfast, we will go to the Areopagus and I will give a reading which will recall some remarkable associations of the place."

The Class quietly followed the thoughtful looking teacher down into a valley on the north of the Acropolis, and up the stone steps to the Areopagus, or old place of justice.

It was a still and sun-flooded morning. There was scarcely a movement to be noticed in the city; almost the only sound to be heard was the occasional tinkling of sheep bells from the neighboring hills. The Acropolis seemed to be tinged with a fiery, golden lustre; to stand out with a strange mysterious distinctness in the bright air.

"More than two thousand years ago," said Master Lewis, "when all the temples you now see were the perfection of art and beauty, there lived at Athens the most wonderful man of Greece, and perhaps the most remarkable of ancient history. His father was a sculptor; he himself was educated to follow his father's profession, and for a time applied himself to the art.

"He could not tell how it was, but he thought that his life had somehow a higher mission than that of other men. He fancied he heard a divine voice calling him. He walked the streets of Athens, continually talking to the unlearned and the wise, the poor and the rich, the market people and people of rank. He was very humble, and he was one day astonished by being told that the Delphic oracle had said that in all the world there was none so wise as he.

"He declared that the soul of man is immortal, and that virtue

THE TEMPLE OF ZEUS, OLYMPIA.

will be rewarded in a future state; that this life is but the beginning of the life of thought and aspiration within. This noble belief was ever present with him and influenced his whole conduct. 'It is our duty,' he said, 'not to return an injury or to do evil to any man.'

"In the year 399 B.C. this great and good man was accused 'of not worshipping the gods whom this city worships,' and of leading the youth to follow his example, and was condemned to die. He was cast into a prison, where he awaited death thirty days.

"*There*," continued Master Lewis, rising and pointing across a deserted hollow, "are the ruins of the prison in which he was confined. *Here*, where you are sitting, he once stood and taught the people.

"He was condemned to drink a cup of poison-hemlock that produces the stupor of death. He received the sentence with his accustomed loftiness of character, saying that death would not end his life, and that he did not fear to meet the change.

"On the last day of his life he uttered a grand discourse on immortality. He said:—

"'Were I not convinced that I shall go into the presence of the wise and good deities, and of departed men better than those on earth, I should do wrong not to be reluctant to die. I am confident as I can be of anything that I shall go to the celestial divinities, and that it will be better with the good than with the wicked after death.'

"He calmly drank the poison. Of all heathen philosophers he most nearly discovered the essential doctrines of the Christian truth.

"Who was he?"

"SOCRATES," answered several voices.

"Can we visit his prison?" they asked.

"I will go to it with you by and by.

"And now let me tell you another story.

"About eighteen hundred years ago there came to Athens, by the way of Thessalonica and Berea, a great missionary. He had been converted near Damascus by a light shining around him that exceeded the brightness of the sun, and by a celestial voice speaking to him. He came and stood upon the place where we are now, 'in the midst of Mars' Hill.'

"The temples that filled all Athens were then in their glory. The statues of deities and heroes rose on every hand. He lifted his eye to the Acropolis and saw the gigantic statue of Minerva shining in the sun. *There* rose the temple of Jupiter Olympus, *yonder* the Theseum. Standing where we now are he uttered one of the grandest discourses that ever fell from human lips. I will read it: —

"Ye men of Athens, I perceive that in all things ye are too superstitious.

"For as I passed by, and beheld your devotions, I found an altar with this inscription, 'TO THE UNKNOWN GOD!' Whom therefore ye ignorantly worship, him declare I unto you.

"God that made the world and all things therein, seeing that he is Lord of heaven and earth, dwelleth not in temples made with hands:

"Neither is worshipped with men's hands, as though he needed anything, seeing he giveth to all life, and breath, and all things;

"And hath made of one blood all nations of men for to dwell on all the face of the earth, and hath determined the times before appointed, and the bounds of their habitation;

"That they should seek the Lord, if haply they might feel after him and find him, though he be not far from every one of us:

"For in him we live, and move, and have our being; as certain also of your own poets have said, 'For we are also his offspring.'

"Forasmuch then as we are the offspring of God, we ought not to think that the godhead is like unto gold, or silver, or stone, graven by art and man's device.

"And the times of this ignorance God winked at; but now commandeth all men everywhere to repent:

"Because he hath appointed a day in the which he will judge the world in righteousness by that man whom he hath ordained; whereof he hath given assurance unto all men, in that he hath raised him from the dead."

"You all know the name of that great missionary. We will now go to the prison of Socrates."

TO PARNASSUS.

From Athens the Class on this memorable excursion went first to Marathon, riding all the way on horseback amid the grandest mountain scenery, and stopping, after a ten hours' journey, to view the mound of the one hundred and ninety-two Greek heroes who fell in the celebrated battle. The night was passed at Marathon. The next day the Class made a fifteen hours' journey to Thebes, which was found to be but a poor town, with scarcely a trace of its magnificence thousands of years ago. From Thebes, on the following morning, the tourists went to Platæa, which was a ruin two thousand years ago, when one of the Greek comic poets said it could boast of only "two temples, a portico, and its glory."

The route now lay over some picturesque hills to the plain of Leuctra, where the Thebans won their famous victory over the Spartans in the heroic days of Epaminondas; thence to Lebadea, the road ascending a great altitude commanding a view of the magnificent mountain scenery of Parnassus.

The view of Parnassus, as indeed of all the grand mountain scenery on the route, drew away the minds of the Class from the discomforts of horseback riding. Over a level country, with few objects in view, the journey would have been fatiguing in the extreme.

When the Greek attendants first pointed out to Master Lewis the triple peaks of Parnassus, and he communicated the information to the boys, Tommy Toby said : —

"Restrain yourselves as much as you can. I shall exact a forfeit of any one who quotes a certain line of poetry."

"What is it?" asked Charlie Leland.

"It begins with 'O.'"

"I am sure I shall be able to restrain myself," said George Howe. "Do you want to know of what I am thinking?"

"Do not go to moralizing and saying anything about America or American institutions in this great and glorious country."

"Great and glorious country! Now, you know that you have not seen a decent road since you came to Greece. The fact is we are living in the past and looking at mountain tops, but we are travelling on horseback over roads that in America would not be regarded as decent cow-paths. There are but two decent streets in Athens, with all its ruins of temples. And what kind of people did we see there?"

"The descendants of heroes," said Tommy.

"A long way descended, I should think. Just think of it! here we are talking of Epaminondas and Agamemnon, and all the rest of 'em, and looking into the air and telling stories about the gods, when we have n't seen a hotel or hardly a respectable shelter since we left Athens. I would give more for a good railroad than for the whole of the Acropolis. Look at our attendants! why, those men know but little more than the horses they drive!"

"It is well they can't understand you," said Charlie.

Just at this point Wyllys Wynn, who had been lagging behind, came trotting up, saying, —

"'O thou Par—'"

"*That* is forbidden," said Tommy.

As the tourists were proceeding on their way after George Howe's very disrespectful remarks about the roads, the gods, and the heroes, a very amusing incident occurred. George had shifted from a horse to a mule. The party was fording a stream; the heat was great, and the journey had become wearisome. When George's mule had partly crossed the stream, it suddenly dropped on its knees and *rolled over*, pitching its rider headlong into the water.

The whole party laughed, as George was unhurt.

"That's what one gets for being disrespectful to Epaminondas and Apollo," said Tommy.

Lebadea; Chæronea, the place of Plutarch; back to Lebadea; Chryse, with awe inspiring views of Mt. Parnassus; DELPHI!

This town, called also Castri, is situated on a lofty eminence on the south side of Parnassus, beneath some perpendicular precipices through which flows the Castalian fountain on its way to the sea. The precipice above this fountain is two thousand feet high. The boys at first thought that these precipices were the summits of the mountain.

The town contained some good houses and an accommodation for travellers. The Class were too weary, when the public house was reached, to enjoy the majestic scenery around, above, and beneath them.

But the morning brought a revelation. Such a scene of majesty and beauty had never opened to the young tourists' minds or fancy. The temple of Apollo, whose oracle decided the fate of nations, was gone, and the three thousand statues that had once adorned the temples and streets of the city had wholly disappeared. But Nature was as glorious as when the oracle spoke there, and the world listened in awe. Heights mantled in purple and gold, and skirted with olive groves; walls that seemed to reach to the very heavens; sharp crags, rocky slopes retreating into distances beyond the reach of the eye, and the eternal cascade fed by the spring snows of Parnassus, — all kindled the eye, bated the breath, and filled the heart with emotions such as only the nobler scenes in life call into being.

"It is worth years of effort to see a scene like this," said Master Lewis, looking down upon a valley of wonderful beauty, and up the rocky cliffs and stairways that seemed like royal passages to the sky. "I do not wonder that the uninspired Greeks thought that this was the abode of the gods!"

Early in the morning the Class left Delphi for the summit of Parnassus, passing up a zigzag path to a considerable height.

"This is what I call climbing," said Tommy.

"Climbing Parnassus," said Wyllys.

"If poets have to climb like this, they earn their honors," said Tommy. "But never mind, we are almost there. I can see the plateau."

"Almost where?" asked Master Lewis.

"At the top."

A little farther on, Tommy, who was riding ahead, exclaimed, —

"Oh! There is the mountain now; why, we have only been climbing up the base. I thought this plain was the top.

"'O thou Parnassus whom I *now* survey,'" continued Tommy, quoting the line he requested the others not to repeat.

The plain was several miles across. The Class after passing over the level rested in a strange cavern called the Corycian Cave, or Forty Courts, which it is said will hold three thousand people. The inhabitants of Delphi took refuge here at the time of the Persian invasion.

The Class crossed another plain, and then beheld the central cone of Parnassus, rising from a base bordered with magnificent pines; a very world of stone shining resplendent in the transparent air.

"How long will it take to ascend?" asked Master Lewis of the guide.

"About five hours."

Height after height was reached, but still the highest peak was far away. Think of going up Mt. Washington, and then finding other heights lifting themselves, platform above platform, two thousand feet higher than the Tiptop House, into the clear air.

"*Hic opus est*," said Tommy.

"*Hic labor est*," said Master Lewis.

An English family were stopping at Delphi, tourists, who had come on horseback or muleback from Athens. There were two young ladies in the family who wished to ascend Mt. Parnassus in company with Master Lewis. They started out from Delphi, receiving every aid and attention from the Greek attendants and guides, who pushed and pulled their mules up steep places; but they at last found Parnassus too hard to climb, and returned to the town. Charlie Leland, also, who did not like the looks of the way up the cone of Parnassus, after one very discouraging stage of the ascent, returned to Castri with the ladies.

Often the party stopped to rest, and looked over Attica which seemed like an ocean of rolling hills. As often the expressions "glorious," "grand," fell from the lips of one or another, and these expressions grew more emphatic as height after height was gained.

PARNASSUS! At last the Class had reached the top, the very seat of Apollo, and, as the god was supposed to have done, looked down upon the world.

What a scene was spread out beneath them! The Gulf of Corinth, which had shone so resplendently in the sun during a part of the journey, now looked no larger than the basin of Versailles or a lakelet before a château. Here was the fabled abode of Apollo: but what lofty heights were those far in the north wearing coronets of silver? It was Olympus, the throne of Jupiter himself. All Greece was mapped before the eye, — a sea of mountains; Helicon, and the glorious peaks of the

MODERN FESTIVAL AT THE TEMPLE OF JUPITER.

Peloponnesus. The Ægean and Ionian seas glimmer like lakes in the horizon, and Pindus is seen winding through Epirus like a ribbon of silver.

This was Parnassus, the most glorious sight ever seen by the human eye; the perfection of the beauty of Nature in all the earth; a throne eight thousand feet high, and one indeed worthy of a poet's divinity.

The Class passed the night at Delphi, and there rested on the following day, when, at Master Lewis's suggestion, the boys made careful notes of their journey. Several of the Class submitted these notes to Master Lewis for correction.

George Howe began his entry in his journal with some practical statements: —

DELPHI, June.

"Have been up Parnassus to see Apollo. He was not at home; had moved; gone to parts unknown. The outlook from the mountain was magnificent; I never expect to see the like again. But, except the grand scenery, Greece is a country of fancy, mapped in the air. There is no enterprise here, no intelligence. I would rather be an engineer on a locomotive than king of Greece."

Charlie Leland's notes needed some revision. They began, —

DELPHI, June.

"I am here. There is a spring here called the Castalian Spring, where Apollo and the Muses were said to come down to drink. The Delphic oracle was here. The priestess's name was Pythia; they gave her a tripod, and she inhaled the smoke and it made her crazy. Then she used to prophesy."

"What is a tripod?" asked Master Lewis.

"I do not know. I thought it was something like a teapot."

"Oh, no! The priestess sat upon a tripod, after inhaling the vapor that ascended from the earth, and then delivered the oracle in rhyme."

Wyllys Wynn wrote, —

AT THE CASTALIAN SPRING.

At Delphi we rest, once the home of the sages,
The moonlight is fair o'er Corinthia's plains,
And fair is Parnassus's brow, that the pages
Of Homer adore in melodious strains.
   But a Voice whispers — Gone,
      Gone, gone!
The olden-time heroes from Hellas have gone!

The night still is glorious, the silver haze drifting,
The Bay of Lepanto with tempered light fills;
And the golden-wheeled moon still is silently lifting
The Goddess of Night o'er the Procian hills.
   But a Voice whispers — Gone,
      Gone, gone!
The olden-time heroes from Hellas have gone!

O night-shaded mount! the Castalian streams tremble,
As in those bright ages by olden bards sung,
When the diademed Nine here were wont to assemble
And list to sweet Clio's and Orpheus' tongue.
   But a Voice whispers — Gone,
      Gone, gone!
The olden-time heroes from Hellas have gone!

And here on these wooded slopes silently lying,
And on the far hills that the ocean intone,
And in the lone vales of the myrtle trees sighing,
The old nations rest from their warfares unknown.
   And a voice whispers — Gone!
      Gone, gone!
The olden-time heroes from Hellas have gone!

The warm airs of springtime embed them with flowers,
The vineyards above them to clustered wine turn;
The nightingales chant in the sun-kindled bowers,
The laurel groves blossom, the palm seasons burn.
   But a voice whispers — Gone,
      Gone, gone!
The olden-time heroes from Hellas have gone!

> But still to great hearts those old heroes are calling,
> The deed of Leonidas marches through time;
> And Epaminondas, upon his shield falling,
> Eternally lives in example sublime.
>   The Voice says, They live,
>   Live, live!
> The olden-time heroes eternally live!
>
> They live in the heart of the new generations,
> They wing the high purpose, they breathe in the breath;
> 'Tis Pericles moulds the grand laws of the nations
> That rise from the ashes of Tyranny's death.
>   The Voice says They live,
>   Live, live!
> The olden-time heroes eternally live!
>
> And Phidias is breathing in art and in story,
> He touches the quarry, the white marbles bloom;
> And Socrates lives, and till ages are hoary
> Will hold the bright taper of hope o'er the tomb.
>   The Voice says, They live,
>   Live, live!
> The olden-time heroes eternally live!

"That is somewhat musical," said Master Lewis; "the thought seems to me a correct one, but the expression is rather sophomoric. Still, I am glad your poetic taste has been stimulated."

The Class returned to Athens. Its next excursion was by steamer to Abydos, where they saw the desolate coast on which "lofty Troy" once stood. Truly the simple Latin sentence expresses the history of the city, *Troja fuit*, — "Troy was." Mt. Ida was seen towering to the clear sky, reminding the Class of the adventures both of Ulysses and Æneas.

On returning to Athens the Class again visited the Acropolis and the ruins of the Temple of Jupiter. At the latter ruin the Greeks still hold festivals, — light, shabby affairs in comparison with the splendid and stately processions of the olden time. Early in July the Class sailed from Athens for Messina.

MESSINA.

CHAPTER X.

THE LANDS OF VULCAN AND CYCLOPS.

SICILY. — MESSINA. — STORY OF ARION AND THE DOLPHIN. — VULCAN'S FORGES. — STORIES OF ERUPTIONS OF ÆTNA. — CATANIA. — PALERMO. — STORY OF THE "SICILIAN VESPERS." — MONREALE. — STORY OF POLYPHEMUS THE GIANT. — THE DEAD PRINCE. — NAPLES.

"THE heat is becoming so great," said Master Lewis, as the Class was entering the Straits of Messina on one of the superb *Messageries Imperiales*, or Marseilles steamers, " that our visit in Sicily must be confined to the coast, chiefly to Messina and Palermo."

It was deliciously cool on the decks of the grand steamer, as she approached the port. The whole city of Messina glittered in the sun. The harbor was a forest of masts, from which dropped many colored pennons; for the Straits of Messina is the highway of the traffic of the Old World from Britain, France, Spain, and Italy to the East, and the delightful port is the bazaar of Europe and the Levant. Around the city were picturesque hills luxuriantly clad with vegetation and graced with villages, chapels, convents, and casinos, and behind the hills rose mountains whose slopes were like gardens stretching to the sky; and behind all towered Ætna, at a distance of fifty miles, piercing the blue vault with its snowy peak eleven thousand feet high.

"Sicily is the toe of the boot of Italy," said Tommy Toby, "and Nature seems all sticking out at the toe."

"Proserpine used to come to Sicily to gather garlands," said Wyllys, "because here were the fairest wild-flowers on earth."

"Who was Proserpine?" asked Charlie Leland.

"She was the Queen of Hades, or the regions *down below*."

"I thought Hades was a dreadful place," said Charlie. "Did Proserpine used to come up from Hades to pick flowers?"

"No," said Tommy, "she was picking flowers when one of the grim gods of Pluto came along and carried her off to Hades."

Sicily, with its serene deep-blue sky, its great volcanoes, its thousands of acres of orange, lemon, and citron groves, its classic antiquities and beautiful churches, is one of the loveliest islands on earth.

In summer the heat is intense, but a breeze from the Mediterranean usually comes stealing through the orange trees about ten o'clock each morning, and cools the air during the rest of the day. The morning and evening air is delicious, and night is an enchantment, a spell,— a starry splendor above, a sea of perfume below.

The Greek and Latin poets were inspired by both the charms and the grandeurs of the Sicilian scenery, and made these shores the scenes of some of their most beautiful and most terrible fables.

Master Lewis related two of these fables to the Class, as follows:

ARION AND THE DOLPHIN.

"It was from Sicily that Arion was sailing when he was rescued from death by the dolphin.

"Arion was a bard, and the inventor of dithyrambic poetry, or festal Greek song.

"He was a sweet player upon the lyre, and his musical skill was the pride of Corinth.

"He went to Sicily to attend a musical assembly, and to take part in a great musical contest. He enchanted the Sicilians, won splendid prizes, and, loaded with presents, took ship for Corinth.

"The sailors coveted his treasures, and laid a plan for his murder. He came to a knowledge of their purpose, and begged leave to be allowed to play upon his lyre once more. The permission was granted him.

"He arrayed himself in festal attire, and with his lyre in his hand placed himself on the prow of the ship, and looking up to the blue sky invoked the help of the gods in enchanting music. He played so sweetly that the dolphins came around the ship to listen.

"When he had ended his song, he cast himself into the sea. A dolphin received him on its back and carried him over the purple waves to Corinth. The sailors were severely punished, when they reached the city, for their purpose to murder the bard."

VULCAN'S FORGES.

"The Volcanic islands about Sicily and Ætna were Vulcan's workshops. The Cyclops were his smiths.

"Vulcan, the god of fire, was the son of Zeus and Hera. He was born lame, and moreover was not a handsome boy; so his mother threw him down from the top of Mt. Olympus, and he fell into the sea. He lived in a grotto of the sea nine years, and then ascended to Olympus. He here offended Zeus his father, and the king of the gods followed the bad example of Vulcan's mother and threw him down from Olympus. He was a whole day in falling, and he must have made a rather zigzag journey on his way, for he alighted on the island of Lemnos, and seems after his misfortune to have been lamer than ever. He was permitted to return to Olympus, however, where he built beautiful palaces for the gods, and also made one for himself which shone like the stars. It contained his workshop, with his anvil and forge, which was kept alive by twenty

WAVES OF VOLCANIC FIRE.

bellows which worked themselves. When on earth he dwelt at Lemnos, Lipari, and Sicily. Polyphemus, the man-eating giant from whom Ulysses escaped, was one of his workmen."

Although Messina is the second city in Sicily, and is even more beautiful than Genoa when viewed from the sea, the Class found little to detain it there. The cathedral, built by the direction of Roger the Norman, the beautiful square and fountain in front of the cathedral, and the viceroy's palace and its promenades were the principal attractions. The mid-day heat was very oppressive, and Master Lewis decided to make a railway trip to Catania at the base of Mt. Ætna, and then to sail from Messina to Palermo.

"Shall we not ascend Mt. Ætna?" asked Tommy.

"I think not. We must go to Rome as soon as possible. The unhealthy season is near, and it would not be safe to risk the consequences of the fatigue of an ascent of Mt. Ætna."

"If we cannot go to the summit of Ætna," said Tommy, "please tell us something about its eruptions, now that it is in view. I like to hear stories of earthquakes and burning mountains. What would you do if Ætna were to begin now to rumble and blaze?"

"From what I know of its history, I should fly to the nearest steamer, and not stop to get my baggage or settle my hotel bill," said Master Lewis. "It is only about a hundred years ago that a disturbance of Ætna threw down the cathedral."

"Here?"

"Yes, in Messina. Nearly all the houses were thrown down; the earth was convulsed and upheaved for an area of five hundred square miles."

"Were many persons killed?"

"It is estimated that forty thousand persons perished at the instant of the earthquake, and twenty thousand from the effects of it.

"On the night of the 20th of August, 1852, a party of English tourists consisting of three gentlemen and three ladies attempted to ascend the mountain, hoping to reach the summit in time to see the sun rise. As they were proceeding on their way, the crater began to pour volumes of fire into the air. It was night, and the sight was

MT. ÆTNA.

awful in the extreme. The party fled to a defile, when a wind came rushing down the mountain, overthrowing the mules, and carrying the whole party some distance towards a steep precipice. They found a shelter in some masses of lava, and clung to it for protection from the wind. Suddenly an earthquake shook the whole mountain. The mules fled in terror, and the next morning the party made their

LAVA-BEDS OF MT. ÆTNA.

way on foot to the nearest town. The mountain poured forth lava, which ran in great streams down its sides threatening the towns for miles around its base."

"How often do eruptions take place?" asked Charlie.

"The history of the eruptions of Ætna," said Master Lewis, "would fill volumes. Pindar, nearly five hundred years before Christ, speaks of 'Ætna, the pillar of heaven, the nurse of the snow, from whose recesses are vomited fountains of unapproachable fire, — rivers

THE HEADLAND OF CAPE D'ALESSIO.

that by day smoke and by night flame, bearing down rocks with a crashing sound to the deep sea.' Sometimes the volcano has been quiet for two hundred years. Then its eruptions have continued for months. In 1169 the people of Catania, near the base of Ætna, filled the cathedral to celebrate the Feast of St. Agatha. Suddenly the volcano shook the island. The cathedral came tumbling down, crush-

CATHEDRAL OF PALERMO.

ing the people within. The town was a heap of ruins; fifteen thousand people perished. In 1669 the craters poured out lava which ran rapidly down the sides of the mountain and reached Belpasso, a town of eight thousand inhabitants, submerging it in a sea of fire. Other eruptions followed; fifty square miles were covered with lava, in some

TAORMINA.

parts one hundred feet deep. Twenty-seven thousand dwellings were destroyed. We have the history of seventy-six terrible eruptions in some two thousand years."

"Where does the fire come from?" asked Charlie.

"From the interior of the earth."

"What is it that feeds those fires two thousand years?"

"I cannot tell. It is one of Nature's appalling mysteries."

The railway to Catania winds between the sea and the mountains. The sea was flooded with sunshine and the land embedded in flowers as the Class was swept along, passing in view of the lofty castle on the headland of Cape d'Alessio, and of Taormina, celebrated for its beauty and its ruins.

WEST PORCH OF THE CATHEDRAL, PALERMO.

The way passed through the region where lived Polyphemus, the one-eyed giant. On the coast were shown the lava rocks, or islands, which the giant is said to have thrown at Ulysses when he found that the latter was escaping by the sea. A beautiful castle, called Aci Castello, rising above these rocks, added picturesqueness to the scene of the story.

Catania is some twenty miles from Ætna. It is situated on a lava formation, and is built of that material. Ætna rises behind it, filling half the horizon. It was an astonishment to the Class to find so splendid a city, with more than sixty thousand inhabitants, in so dangerous a situation.

LAVA STREAMS.

The view of Ætna from this city is majestic, but the mid-day heat was great, though somewhat abated by the cool winds of the sea.

The distance from Messina to Palermo is about one hundred and thirty miles. The Class found the sail very delightful, over a sea commanding the most enchanting prospects, and beneath a sky of rarest serenity and loveliness.

Palermo, a city of churches, walled with mountains!—so appears the scene as one approaches the city from the sea. The place contains nearly two hundred thousand inhabitants. There are about two hundred churches in Palermo, but the cathedral is its crowning architectural glory.

Near Palermo is a lovely plain covered with gardens. It was once an esplanade. In this place is an old Norman church dedicated to the Holy Ghost. This site will ever be memorable as the scene of one of the great tragedies of history.

SOUTH PORCH OF THE CATHEDRAL, PALERMO.

ACI CASTELLO.

THE SICILIAN VESPERS.

It was Easter Tuesday, 1282. The esplanade was carpeted with flowers, and over it the Sicilians were passing on their way to the Resurrection Festival.

The French had long ruled Sicily with an iron hand. The Sicilians, whenever they assembled on any public occasion, were sure to be reminded of their servile and crushed condition by the appearance of their French masters among them. They burned with a patriotic ardor to throw off the rule of their oppressors, and only awaited the opportunity.

Lent had passed, and on this day the gay Sicilian character was exhibited in the festival. They danced, they feasted socially from little tables spread on the grass. It seemed like the old days of their rustic peace and freedom.

Suddenly the French officers appeared among them, insolent, dictatorial; coming, as they claimed, to preserve order. The happiness vanished, and fierce anger filled every Sicilian's heart.

At last a Frenchman offered an insult to a lady, who fell fainting in terror at his words and impudent conduct.

"Death to the French!" shouted the husband of the injured woman.

A young Sicilian sprang upon the offending French soldier, and killed him.

"Death to the French!" shouted the people.

The Sicilians slew two hundred French people on the spot. The tables arranged for the festival were covered with blood. The crowd armed themselves with the weapons of those they had overcome.

"Death to the French!"

It was nightfall. The victorious Sicilians came rushing into Palermo, striking down every French person they met. The French people rushed to the holy altars, but the Sicilians followed them there, and reddened the churches with blood.

> "The startled monks thronged up
>   In the torchlight cold and dim,
> And the priest let fall his incense cup,
>   And the virgin hushed her hymn;
> For a boding clash, and a clanging tramp,
>   And a summoning voice was heard,
> And fretted wall and tombstone damp
>   To the fearful echo stirred.
>
> "The peasant heard the sound
>   As he sat beside his hearth,
> And the song and dance were hushed around,
>   And the fireside tale of mirth;
> The chieftain shook in his bannered hall
>   As the sound of war drew nigh,
> And the warder shrank from the castle wall
>   As the gleam of spears went by.
>
> "Proud beings fell that hour,
>   The young and passing fair,
> And the flame went up from dome and tower, —
>   The avenger's arm was there!
> For the wakened pride of an injured land
>   Had burst its iron thrall —
> From the plumèd chief to the pilgrim band,
>   Woe, woe to the sons of Saul!"

A night of slaughter followed. Two thousand French people fell.

> "The morning sun with a quiet smile
>   Looked out o'er hill and glen,
> O'er ruined temple and mouldering pile,
>   And the ghastly forms of men.

> "Ay, the sunshine sweetly smiled
> As its early glance came forth :
> It had no sympathy with the wild
> And terrible things of earth ;
> And the man of blood that day might read,
> In language freely given,
> How ill his dark and midnight deed
> Became the light of heaven."

The massacre is known in history as "The Sicilian Vespers."

The plain of Palermo has been called an earthly paradise, and is certainly one of the most beautiful in the world. Across it, on a

THE CATHEDRAL OF MONREALE.

picturesque elevation, stands Monreale, an ecclesiastical town, with its old cathedral, the finest in Sicily.

The Class made their way to Monreale early in the morning, in order to avoid the mid-day heats. The distance was four miles. The boys had never seen before such a beautiful road as this. Gardens of

WESTERN PORCH, CATHEDRAL OF MONREALE.

olives, almonds, and oranges; fountains shaded by cypresses and graced with statuary; Latin inscriptions on old walls, piles of flowers bursting from every rocky crevice and ruin, scattering odors on every breeze,

CLOISTERS OF THE CATHEDRAL OF MONREALE.

— all made this walk, next to the view from Parnassus, the most delightful event of their journey.

The cathedral of Monreale has been rising and growing for centuries, and the artists of many lands and schools have lavished their genius as the Sicilians have bestowed their wealth upon it. The portals display the most elaborate carving, and the open cloister is almost as delicate and superbly graceful as any court of the Alhambra.

The view of Palermo from Monreale is one of peculiar beauty. Descending to the plain one passes an unbroken mass of orange groves

THE PALACE OF LA ZIZA.

for nearly a mile. Among the surprises that one meets on the way is the quaint old palace of La Ziza, a relic of the times of the Saracens.

The Class spent three days at Palermo. The heat was so great during the last two days as to compel the boys to remain in the hotel during the middle of the day. The windows were shaded, and, as all exercise was to be avoided, Charlie Leland proposed that they should have in these mid-day hours a literary meeting of the Zigzag Club.

"An informal one," said Master Lewis.

"I will ask questions," said Charlie, "as I am the youngest member, and the other and more learned members can answer."

"Well, what would you like to know?" asked Master Lewis.

"Something more about Polyphemus, the big giant."

"Tommy can answer that. I saw him reading a pony Virgil this morning."

THE GIANT POLYPHEMUS.

"Well, —

"Troy fell when the wooden horse came into the city, and Priam and his brave sons and weak son perished in the siege and overthrow.

"There was a prince of Troy named Æneas, whose mother was said to be the goddess Venus. When the city was overthrown he took his old father on his back, and with his family and a band of Trojans escaped to Mt. Ida, where he caused ships to be built, and whence he and his followers set out to discover an unknown land which Venus had promised, where he might found a new Troy.

"He sailed along the coast of the Mediterranean over the way we have been passing, and his adventures were for the most part a repetition of those of Ulysses.

"Æneas, however, did not attempt to pass through the Straits of Messina, then known as Scylla and Charybdis, but sailed around the south coast of Sicily.

"When he was near the foot of Mt. Ætna a very strange incident happened. A man came running down to the beach hailing the ship, and begging to be taken on board.

"To the surprise of the Trojans this man proved to be a Greek. He was one of the companions of Ulysses, and had been captured by the one-eyed giant Polyphemus and shut up with the other Greeks in the monster's cave. When the others escaped from the island he had become separated from them and left behind. He had lived in the forests since that time. The giant being blind could not find him now, and he had been hoping for some chance to escape from the region.

"The Trojans took the man on board one of their boats, and were rejoicing over his recovery, when a frightful spectacle presented itself to their sight.

"Over the lava hills came a tall man, a mountain of flesh, with an enormous head, and holding a pine tree in his hand, which he used for a cane.

"He had no eyes. There was a great cavity in the middle of his forehead. The Greek who had been taken on board recognized him, you may be sure. It was Polyphemus. He was coming down to the sea to bathe the cavity where his one eye had been. The Trojans rowed away with great terror."

"Do you really think there ever was such a man as Polyphemus?" asked Charlie Leland.

"Ask such a question as that, when you have just seen the rocks he tossed into the sea after Ulysses!" said Tommy.

"Yes, but fifty yoke of oxen could not move one of those rocks."

"That shows how great a man Polyphemus must have been," said Tommy.

"What do you think about Polyphemus, Master Lewis?" asked Charlie.

"I think it all a fable. But the skeletons of gigantic men have been found in Sicily; so the fable may have been suggested by a race of men of great stature who lived here in early times."

Master Lewis continued the impromptu entertainment by reading "The Sicilian's Tale," from Longfellow's "Wayside Inn," —

"Robert of Sicily, brother of Pope Urbane
And Valmond, Emperor of Allemaine," etc.

"Who was Robert of Sicily?" asked Charlie.

"Now you have asked a question equal to the Sphinx's riddle," said Master Lewis.

"He was brother of Pope Urbane," said Tommy.

"And Valmond, Emperor of Allemaine," said Wyllys.

"Who was Pope Urbane?" asked Charlie.

"It is your turn to answer," said Master Lewis, to Tommy. "I am sure I do not know. I am afraid the poet took a large poetic license in these two lines."

"What was the Sphinx's riddle?" asked Charlie.

"The Sphinx used to catch a poor Theban, and ask him a certain question. If he could answer he was allowed to go free; if not, she ate him up. Who can tell the story of the Sphinx?"

None of the Class were able.

"Suppose you look up the matter, Tommy," said Master Lewis, "and tell us the story at some other time."

Mr. Beal related the Story of "Robert the Devil," the father of William the Conqueror, whose history is associated with Sicily, in popular traditions.

Wyllys Wynn had a poem in his note-book which he had written a year before when in Normandy, amid the associations of the history of William the Conqueror. He had since revised it. He contributed it as his part of the entertainment: —

THE DEAD PRINCE.

Oh, light was the heart of Duke William,
    The minstrels all playing with glee,
His fleet dancing bright on the Channel,
    And Normandy sunk in the sea;
Above him, the sky of September,
    Below him, the waters at rest,
And snowy sails breaking around him
    The light of the opaline west:
The thousand ships dropping their pennons,
    The gonfalons waving in view,
His ensign, the Normandy Lions,
    Rolled out from the mast in the blue.
"Do you see," said the Duke to the nobles,
    "The green island rising afar?
Its forests are broader and fairer
    Than those of old Normandy are.
A thousand prows cleaving the ocean
    Ten thousand men bear to the foe,
And soon in yon forests the hunters
    The Normandy bugle shall blow."

Oh, hard was the battle that followed!
  The Normans, as reddened the air
The moon of the golden September,
  Bowed down on the meadows in prayer:
They sang the great war-song of Roland
  When morning uplifted its light,
And the Three Norman Lions victorious
  Waved over the carnage at night.
The standards of England were taken
  'Mid plumed arrows falling like rain,
And King Harold, discrowned and forsaken,
  Was found in heaps of the slain.

Then rose the conqueror's palace
  On Winchester's circle of hills,
Where the stag bounded over the woodlands
  And bright watercourses and rills;
But all the great forests were broken
  By hamlets and villages rude,
And the ivy-clad fane of the Saxon
  Uplifted its cross in the wood.
Then the conqueror said: "In the cottage
  The rabbit a burrow shall make,
And the deer shall bound over the village
  As free as the bird on the lake;
And Richard, my noble boy Richard,
  Who the crown of dead Harold shall wear,
And who loves the wild chase in the forests,
  Shall oft lead the noblemen there!"

He touched the red torch to the hamlet,
  He touched the red torch to the fane,
And the peasants went forth from the forest
  To behold it never again.
Oh, then there were weeping and wailing!
  Oh, then there was wringing of hands!
There was blood in the desolate rivers,
  There was smoke in the desolate lands:
The peasants looked back on the forests,
  And cried, in their helplessness wild, —
"May the curse of God blight the oppressor!
  May the curse of God visit his child!"
He was cursed by the widow and orphan
  As they stood by the graves of the slain,
He was cursed by old Aldred the bishop,
  As his army swept over the plain.

EDITH DISCOVERS THE BODY OF HAROLD.

ARCHBISHOP ALDRED'S CURSE.

But over the Thames and the Severn,
  And over Humber and Dee,
From the Cape of the North to the Channel
  Waved the Lions of Normandy three.

It was night at the ending of summer,
  It was night, and the forests were still,
Save when the wild horn of the hunter
  Rang out from the cliff and the hill, —
And gaily Prince Richard had feasted
  When morning illumined the East,
And dashed into the heart of the forest
  Right merrily after the feast.
'Twas night: the great moon was ascending,
  Illuming the tops of the wood,
When the noblemen found in a thicket
  A hunter bedabbled with blood;
They bore the lithe form to King William, —
  The blood on the forehead so fair,
The blood in the dimples of beauty,
  The blood in the tresses of hair!
He wiped the red stains from the forehead,
  He wiped the red gore from the face,
Then folded the form to his bosom
  In a last and impassioned embrace;

Then under the tapestries purple,
    And under the lamps of gold,
He bowed on the dead, and his sorrow
    With tears on his furrowed cheeks told: —

"The fallow deer bounds through the woodland free,
The nest of the heron is safe on the tree,
But here, in the hall of my palace, I see
    My noble boy dead!

"And thou to the sunlight wilt never return,
When the dew of the summer-time jewels the fern,
And over the forests the harvest moons burn, —
    My noble boy dead!

"Oh, bright was my way o'er the slumbering sea,
The gonfalons waving, the minstrels in glee
Played sweet 'neath the Lions of Normandy three, —
    My noble boy dead!

"And bright was the evening, the moon it was round,
The dead and the dying lay thick on the ground,
As I stood by the side of young Harold discrowned, —
    My noble boy dead!

"But what is a sceptre, and what is a crown,
And what is a kingdom of ancient renown,
When the heart is despoiled and the tears trickle down? —
    My noble boy dead!

"I place my hard hand on thy beautiful hair,
I lift thy white fingers so tender and fair,
But thy lips are as mute as the shadowy air, —
    My noble boy dead.

"The shades of the forest are pleasant no more,
Let the peasants return to the hamlets of yore;
I would give the bright crown of the isle to restore
    My noble boy dead!

"I long for my youth, for the heart of a friend,
For the peace of mind only that virtue can lend;
And I long, O my boy! as I over thee bend,
    But to lie in thy stead."

THE LANDS OF VULCAN AND CYCLOPS.   263

A day's sail across the Mediterranean brought the Class in view of Naples and Vesuvius. From the blue Vesuvian bay the city seemed like a splendid assemblage of marble palaces, temples, and stately mansions. But, as in the case of other cities on the Mediterranean, the illusion is dispelled as soon as the foot touches the land. Instead of

STREET SCENE IN NAPLES.

princely inhabitants of white palaces, the Class were astonished to encounter a noisy crowd coarsely laughing or scolding, or abusing insignificant, dispirited looking donkeys. Every other person seemed to be a showman, or a beggar, or a musician in rags.

Tommy Toby and Charlie Leland delayed the whole party on the way to the hotel by loitering behind to admire and patronize an enterprising musician, who supplemented a novel performance on the fiddle by causing three little dogs with hats, ruffles, and curled tails to walk about on two legs, — a feat so interesting as to banish from the boys' minds all thoughts of Vesuvius, or of the stately houses and three hundred churches around them.

"I never saw a sight like this," said Tommy Toby. "People of every nation and color and kind of dress!"

"Look at that fat man with all his baskets on that little donkey," said Charlie. "What a shame! The man looks better able to carry the donkey than the donkey the man. See *him* go! I wish I had such a little animal as that. He is so covered up by the rider you can hardly see him."

There were surprises on every hand.

Splendid vehicles rolled past amid the crowd of donkeys. A military officer flew by, holding his hat on his head with one hand and his bridle in the other, and bounding into the air at every motion of his horse.

"See him *scatter!*" said Charlie. He referred to the horse whose feet seemed to spread out over the street, as though about to kick at every angle.

A MILITARY OFFICER.

Then a beggar without legs was seen mounting a donkey which looked to be less in size than the body of his owner. Two boys were helping the man climb up on the poor little animal's back.

THE LANDS OF VULCAN AND CYCLOPS.

"'See Naples and die!'" said Master Lewis.

"I should think one would die of laughing if one stayed here long," said Tommy.

"How long shall we remain?" asked Charlie.

"Only long enough to visit Pompeii and the tomb of Virgil," said Master Lewis. "We must go as soon as possible to Rome. In the latter part of summer there is danger of the Roman fever, and I wish the Class to make the visit there at once."

CHAPTER XI.

ROME.

A GLANCE AT ROMAN HISTORY. — AN EXPLANATION OF TERMS WHICH TRAVELLERS USE IN SPEAKING OF ROME. — THE DISAPPEARANCE OF ROMULUS. — PLANS FOR FOUR DAYS' EXCURSIONS IN ROME. — THE COLOSSEUM. — A PICTURE OF THE PAST. — ARCH OF CONSTANTINE, — OF SEVERUS. — THE CAPITOL. — ST. PETER'S. — THE VATICAN. — ST. PAUL'S. — THE PANTHEON. — PALATINE HILL. — THE LATERAN. — BATHS OF CARACALLA. — THE CATACOMBS. — CAPUCHIN CHURCH. — STORY-TELLING. — TOMMY GIVES AN ODD VERSION OF THE STORY OF ÆNEAS AND QUEEN DIDO. — MASTER LEWIS'S VIEWS OF THE STUDY OF THE CLASSIC POETS. — THE SPHINX'S RIDDLE. — THE FALL OF ROME. — THE LAST BOW.

I STAND on the Tarpeian Rock; the Tiber is flowing beneath me, the Palatine is dreaming under the purple sky before me. My mind runs back over all I have read of Latin History, and there passes before me the vision of Rome.

"I see Æneas fleeing from the destruction of Troy, and bringing his household gods over the Mediterranean. I see him received by Latinus, and given in marriage to his daughter, — thus beginning the long line of Latin kings. I see Romulus founding Rome and governing it with the senate of a hundred Latin Fathers. The virtuous Numa Pompilius is king. The struggle between the champions of the Romans and Albans, the Horatii and the Curiatii, excites the nation. Tullus is king; Ancus Martius; Tarquinius Priscus; Tullius; Tarquinius Superbus. The Roman republic begins, two consuls being chosen by annual elections. Cincinnatus is called from his plough to save the Republic from her enemies; is victorious, and immediately returns to his farm on the Tiber again. The *Decemviri* or the Ten Consuls; the episode of Virginia. The Gauls come marching over the Alps; they enter the Latin city, and murder the venerable senators as the latter sit like statues in their official seats. Camillus is dictator. Titus Manlius Torquatus re-enacts in history the deed of David, the Hebrew shepherd boy, and becomes champion, consul, dictator. The Samnites conquer Rome, and compel the Romans to pass under the yoke. The Punic wars, or struggles with Carthage; the fall of Carthage, and the rising splendor of Rome.

"Rome is queen now, crowned among the world's cities. Carthage is hers, Corinth is hers; Macedonia, Syracuse. There are grand triumphs in her streets, and her eagles go forth to win universal dominion. The Cæsars complete the conquests which the Republic had begun, and assume the purple of the Emperors.

"The mind sweeps along through a period of imperial pomps. Look at the mile-stones, the names linked to the now dark, now resplendent chronology! Augustus, Tiberius, Caligula, Claudius, Nero, Galba, Othro, Vitellius, Vespasian, Titus, and a long line of assassinated emperors to Constantine, when Rome rules the world. Now the gods of Æneas and Latinus vanish, and Christianity enthrones herself on the hills of the eternal city. The old Rome of ruin, the new Rome of art, and the ecclesiastical Rome of the Papacy follow these half-forgotten scenes. The Rome of two thousand years of tragic history is still shining in the sun, and I am in Rome!

"I sit on the Tarpeian Rock, from whose heights traitors were once hurled in sight of the excited throngs in the Forum. But the Tarpeian Rock of history and poetry is gone. The land has crept up its sides, and one now might leap from its top, were it possible to do so, and alight without destruction. The peaceful garden of the Institute buds and blossoms and grows green around me. This indeed is not the Tarpeian Rock of my school-studies and dreams!"

So Wyllys Wynn wrote in his journal when resting for awhile in the garden of a scientific institute, after making his first day's excursion about Rome. It gives a discursive glance over Roman history, prompted perhaps by guide-book reading; but we can hardly better give an idea of the city to which the Class have at last come than by producing this brief historical sketch.

Before we begin a description of the Class's visits in Rome, there are perhaps some terms that we ought to make clear to the reader.

The *Campagna* is an undulating tract of country surrounded by hills, on which Rome is built.

The *Appian Way* was a road that led from the city to Brundusium, and was built by Appius Claudius more than three hundred years before Christ.

The *Corso* is the principal street of modern Rome.

The *Capitoline* is one of the seven hills of the city; on it was the temple of Jupiter Capitolinus.

The *Palatine* is another of the hills of Rome, and was the original site of the city.

The *Aventine, Esquiline,* and *Quirinal* are also hills of Rome.

The *Campus Martius* was the ancient military field of Rome. The modern city is built upon it. More than two thousand years ago a most extraordinary event is said to have happened in this place.

It was a resplendent day. There was to be a review of the Roman soldiers in the Campus Martius. Romulus, who had reigned thirty-seven years, appeared before the applauding people, full of honor and glory.

The sun was blazing in the sky. Suddenly a shadow seemed creeping over it, and a darkness fell upon the earth. There was a rising wind — a storm — a tempest! The people fled to their homes.

The next day, when daylight came, it was found that Romulus had disappeared in the tempest. It was reported that one had seen Mars descend, or send down a fiery chariot, and bear him away to heaven. Romulus soon afterwards, according to tradition, appeared in the beauty of a god to Proculus Julius, and bade him tell the Romans to honor him as the guardian divinity of Rome.

Such is the story of the poets and mythologists. The more reasonable version was that the senators who were tired of his rule cut him to pieces during the tempest, and each carried away a part of him under his cloak. It would, however, be agreeable to one's taste to believe the poets.

It was Master Lewis's plan to remain with the party one week in Rome; to visit famous places with Mr. Beal and the boys during the

THE ARENA OF THE COLOSSEUM.

first four days, and to rest during the other three days, allowing the boys to seek out such places as best suited their individual tastes. In order that the boys might prepare themselves for the four days' visits by suitable reading, he gave each of them slips of paper containing a programme of the trips about the city that he intended to conduct in person. The programme on each slip was as follows: —

First Day. — Colosseum. Arch of Constantine. Arch of Titus. Roman Forum. Mamertine Prison. The Capitol. Tarpeian Rock.
Second Day. — St. Peter's. The Vatican. Protestant Cemetery. St. Paul's.
Third Day. — The Pantheon. Colosseum again. Palace of the Cæsars. The Lateran.
Fourth Day. — Baths of Caracalla. Catacombs. Circus Maxentius. Quirinal Palace. Capuchin Church.

The Colosseum was the largest theatre the world ever saw, and is now the most imposing ruin in existence. Its associations are almost wholly cruel and wicked, and form some of the darkest chapters in human history. It was built by the bloody emperor Titus; sixty thousand captive Jews were employed upon it ten years. It was baptized in blood: it is said that on the occasion of its dedication five thousand wild beasts and ten thousand captives were slain. The festival on this occasion lasted one hundred days. It then would seat nearly one hundred thousand spectators, and it covered six acres of ground. It was a school of brutal passions, but a structure so grand and vast as to make the emperors who seated themselves there in purple and pomp to feast their eyes on the scenes of suffering and blood feel secure in their vices. Here the early Christians were devoured by wild beasts; here St. Ignatius — the disciple of St. John, the reputed child whom Jesus took in his arms and blessed — met his death.

"We saw nothing in Greece that brings to mind such a dark history as this," said Wyllys Wynn, after listening to an account of the history of the Colosseum which Master Lewis and Mr. Beal had given. "I love Greece, — I mean ancient Greece. I like Homer and all the stories he tells of the gods and heroes. The people seem always to have been doing heroic deeds, or studying morals, or dreaming of the rewards of virtue and an immortal existence. All other histories I have read, except the Bible, are darkness when compared to Greece."

"You are too enthusiastic and partial, my boy," said Mr. Beal. "I too love ancient Greece, and am charmed with Homer's poetry, and with the discoveries of the moral philosophers. But Greece, too, had her vices. The worship of Bacchus prevailed even in the Heroic Age of which the scholar so much likes to dream. Rome exhibited as grand virtues as Greece before the times of the emperors, before she surrendered her liberties to a military chieftain; before Cæsar disobeyed the senate, and crossed the Rubicon."

"Still, Wyllys is nearly right," said Master Lewis. "Ancient Greece is darkened by no period so brutal as that of the Roman emperors.

"Think of the scenes that have been witnessed within these walls! Yonder sat the Roman emperor, surrounded by senators and the beautiful ladies of Rome. The thousands of seats rising tier on tier were filled with the populace in holiday attire, perhaps eighty thousand in number. In the arena below two gladiators appear, with muscles that stand out like iron. They begin a deadly contest; one overcomes the other, and places his foot on his body. The victim looks up to the emperor. All is excitement now. Every one asks the question, 'Will the emperor order his life to be spared?' To do so would be to diminish the full and crowning excitement of the scene. The emperor inverts his thumb as a sign that the vanquished gladiator is to be slain. The *ladies* shriek with delight. The spectators from every gallery thunder applause. The victor plunges his trident into the victim, whose body is drawn out of the arena, leaving a track of blood behind.

"No, Greece in her palmiest days had nothing like this. I, like Wyllys, love Greece for her philosophers and poets. The ancient Greeks were descended from Ion, of the family of Noah; and although they relapsed into idolatry and came to believe in many gods, something that has a pleasing approach to truth is found in all their

ERYTHRÆAN SIBYL, SISTINE CHAPEL.

mythology. The literature of Greece is full of examples of virtue. It glows with a belief in the immortality of the soul, which constitutes its greatest charm."

"Grand as was the Colosseum," said Mr. Beal, "it was as a child in stature as compared with the Circus Maximus, whose ruins still are seen between the Palatine and Avertine Hills. This was so vast as to seat 250,000 people, and a half-million people are said to have witnessed the races at a single exhibition there in the days of Rome's prosperity. The racers were indeed encompassed about with a 'cloud of witnesses.' The spectators, as they looked up from the exciting scenes within the wall, beheld the palaces on the two hills towering in the sunlight above them."

The Class next visited the Arch of Constantine, erected to the memory of the Roman emperor who is said to have been converted to the Christian faith by seeing a cross in the sky, but who seems to have favored Christianity for political reasons, when he found it was becoming triumphant all over the West. He was the first Christian monarch. The arch is adorned with *relievos* and medallions which recite his virtues and deeds of valor. From this arch the Class proceeded to the Arch of Titus, erected to commemorate the fall of Jerusalem. The Jews to this day never pass under this arch.

The Class now passed through the Roman Forum, still beautiful with its surroundings of broken columns and ruined temples, and visited the Mamertine Prison, in which St. Peter and St. Paul are said to have been confined by the order of Nero.

Among the stately ruins of the Roman Forum none so much interested the Class as the Arch of Septimus Severus.

"Who was Septimus Severus?" asked Charlie.

"A Roman conqueror," said Master Lewis.

"Whom did he conquer?"

"The Arabians, Parthians, and Adiabeni. Notice the bas-reliefs on the side which represents his conquests."

"How grand it must have been when it was first erected!" said Charlie.

"Yes," said Master Lewis. "It was indeed grand then. Fine as it is as a ruin, its chief beauties to the old Romans are now gone. In the days of Rome's power and glory it was adorned by a majestic figure of the Emperor, who was represented as being borne through the air on a triumphal car drawn by six noble horses, with a crown of victory on his head. The Forum was then a pile of magnificence, and over it the figure of the Emperor in his chariot, seemingly flying across the top of the arch, shone in the sunlight. None but scholars and travellers ever speak of him now."

After a lunch on the Corso the Class visited the Capitol, situated on the Capitoline Hill. It was the citadel of ancient Rome. From its tower the Class obtained a glorious view of the whole city, and were enabled to trace the Seven Hills on which ancient Rome sat throned in the days of her splendor, when she ruled the world.

On the following morning the Class went to St. Peter's, the most marvellous church in the world. It is built on the place where stood the temple of Jupiter Vaticanus, whence the name of the palace of the Vatican. The first church here is said to have been built A.D. 90. It was a memorial chapel to St. Peter, and was according to tradition erected over the spot where the saint was buried. Constantine built a basilica on the site. The present structure, the glory of the genius of Michael Angelo, was begun about 1503. Its building overtaxed the Christian world; the sale of indulgences to obtain money to spend on the edifice led to the Reformation, and to the loss of Germany and nearly all of the North of Europe to the Roman Church.

The church looks immense in the distance. The piazza with its exquisite columns and cool fountains prepares the mind for the first burst of the expansive majesty and glittering glory of the interior; yet the boys, when their first bewilderment was over, seemed to experience a shade of disappointment as they looked up into the dome.

INTERIOR OF THE COLOSSEUM.

"It is magnificent," said Wyllys; "and yet I thought it was even greater and more impressive. It looked like a mountain when we saw it from the town."

"Observe the cherubs yonder," said Master Lewis. "How large do they seem to be?"

"About as large as dolls," said Wyllys.

"Let us go and see," said Master Lewis. "Or rather let Tommy go and measure one of the cherubs around its leg. We will watch him while he goes."

Tommy crossed the church; as the other boys watched him the distance grew, and seemed a journey. When he reached the cherubs, he too seemed like a doll.

He made the same long journey back.

"How large did you find it?" asked Wyllys.

"Much larger than your body," said Tommy.

"How high do you suppose is the canopy over the altar, and how much do you think it weighs?" asked Master Lewis.

"Fifty feet high, and weighs a ton," said Charlie.

"Nearly one hundred feet high, and weighs nearly one hundred tons," said Master Lewis.

"Yonder is the statue of St. Peter. How high does it seem?" asked Master Lewis.

"Three feet," said Charlie.

"It is twice as large and as tall as a common man," said Master Lewis.

The Class ascended to the dome, and at every step their wonder grew.

"The church is becoming a mountain again," said Wyllys.

The view of Rome from the dome again displayed the magnitude of the church. The people in the streets looked like pigmies. There was a ball on the cross of the dome which was hollow, and in this ball sixteen persons could meet at once.

Next the Vatican was the Papal palace, the grandest picture-gallery in the world. It is said that the Vatican contains thirteen thousand apartments and more than two hundred stairways. It is a little city in itself, and the Sistine Chapel is its own church. It is the residence of the Pope in winter. It contains some of the noblest frescos of Michael Angelo, of which the Last Judgment on the altar-wall of the Sistine Chapel is the most notable.

Among the pictures in the Sistine Chapel those of the sibyls, more than the Scripture scenes, seemed to interest the boys and prompt inquiries.

"I cannot see why Michael Angelo should have represented *sibyls* in a Christian church," said Charlie.

"Listen to a quotation," said Master Lewis: —

> "'Dies irae, dies i'la,
> Solvet sæclum in favilla,
> Teste David cum Sibylla,' —

the last line, translated, meaning, 'Foretold by David and the Sibyl!'"

"I thought the sibyls were fortune-tellers, not prophets," said Charlie.

"Read the Fourth Pastoral of Virgil," said Master Lewis.

"I cannot."

"Read a translation of it in Beattie's works. This Pastoral abounds in the beautiful imagery that Isaiah uses in prefiguring the coming of Christ."

"But Virgil was not a sibyl."

"He is supposed to have obtained inspiration from the leaves of the Cumæan Sibyl. The early Church held Virgil in great esteem. There is a story told that Paul, on his way to Rome, stopped at the tomb of Virgil at Naples, and there expressed his regret that the poet could not have lived to have received the gospel of Christ. This is probably a fable, but the old Latin Church claimed that sibyls, as well

ANCIENT CONSTANTINIAN BASILICA OF ST. PETER'S

as prophets, foretold the coming of an era of imperishable truth, light, and hope to the world."

"Were there other sibyls than the Cumæan?" asked Charlie.

"Yes, the Erythræan; look at her noble figure yonder, — what a splendid face, what a matchless creation of art! There were also the Libyan, the Delphian, and the Babylonian Sibyls. The Sibylline books or prophecies were kept in the Temple of Jupiter, on the Capitoline, and were guarded with great care. Shortly before the Christian era this temple was burned, and most of these remarkable records were thus destroyed."

In a silent and secluded place, near the gate of St. Paul, and close to a lonely pyramid, the Class found the graves of Shelley and Keats. On the tombstone of one was inscribed, "Cor Cordium," — heart of hearts; and on the other tablet was engraved, "Here lies one whose name was writ in water."

About a mile from this spot and from the walls of Rome is a magnificent church with a wonderful history. It was begun by Constantine, who built a basilica on the spot to commemorate the martyrdom of St. Paul at this place. In the fourth century another church was built in its place, and under its altar, according to tradition, St. Paul's remains were interred. This church grew to be the most splendid in Rome. It was nearly destroyed by fire in 1823. Its rebuilding was at once begun; the model of its interior was exceedingly splendid; it was finished after some fifty years' work and dedicated with great pomp, on which occasion were present delegates from the whole Catholic world. A ride to this church from the gate of St. Paul completed the sight-seeing of the Class for the day.

The next day was devoted to the Pantheon and the Palatine Hill. The Pantheon is the best preserved temple of ancient Rome now in existence. It was the admiration of the world eighteen centuries ago, and its portico is still regarded as a marvel of beauty and a model of art. It was changed from a pagan temple to a Christian church when

RUINS OF THE PALACE OF TIBERIUS.

Christianity at last, after the most bloody persecutions the world ever saw, peacefully but triumphantly overturned all the old altars of the Roman world.

ARCH OF CONSTANTINE.

The Palatine Hill!—its history is that of Rome. As we think of it, we seem to see Romulus marking out by a furrow around it the site of the city; the past revives, its figures start into life. Here dwelt the Cæsars, and here are the ruins of their palaces; here dwelt Cicero, Mark Antony, the mother of the Gracchi. Ivies and wall-flowers cover what ruins, what palaces, what shrines! Here were halls of marble mingled with gems; conquerors dwelt here, emperors in purple,— Augustus, Tiberius, Caligula, Claudius. The dust of a thousand years has collected in the broken arches, and the dead palaces to-day are all alive with flowers and perfume. Awful tragedies too were here: but we must shut the book of the past. The Class went from the Palatine to the church where the popes are crowned,— St. John of Lateran, commonly called the Lateran. It is both a church and a museum.

The fourth day's excursions began with a visit to the famous Baths of Caracalla. These immense ruins, a mile in circumference, lie on a plain between the Avertine Hill and the Appian Way. The Baths in the days of the emperors constituted an immense pleasure-house or establishment, consisting of porticos, gardens, an artificial lake, and marble halls rich in coloring, bas-reliefs and statues. The baths proper would accommodate sixteen hundred bathers at a time.

The visit most interesting to the boys which the Class made in Rome was to the Catacombs.

There are many catacombs under Rome, enormous caverns filled with tombs. Some of these may have once been baths or chambers of palaces; many of them contain chapels, and living monks keep company with the dead. Some were once the dens of wild beasts, kept for the bloody spectacles in the colosseum, and many of them were the hiding-places of the Christians in the days of persecution.

The Catacombs that the Class visited were those on the Appian Way, two miles beyond the gate of San Sebastiano. These were the dwelling-places of the early Christians, when their faith was growing and their numbers were multiplying amid restless opposition and fearful slaughter.

A Franciscan monk, himself looking like a spectre, led the Class down into these dismal regions.

"Had I found this place alone," said Wyllys, "I should have thought I had discovered one of the entrances to Hades. It seems like the opening that Homer and Virgil describe, when Ulysses and Æneas went down to the realms of Pluto and the shades."

"How far do these caverns extend?" asked Master Lewis of the ghostly guide.

"They have been explored for *twenty* miles," was the astonishing answer.

The guide carried a torch, and went on, on, into narrow passages full of dull, heavy, lifeless air, into vaulted ways choked up with stones, amid skeletons and graves, — seemingly endless graves. The Class followed in silence.

"Suppose his torch should go out!" whispered Wyllys.

"We should never behold the open air again," said Tommy.

Just then the ghostly guide stumbled.

Charlie Leland began to cry, and said: —

"I want to go back. It is dreadful! How do we know that we are not being led to some place of murderers or thieves?"

On, on went the guide, amid the graves of the martyrs, through streets and alleys innumerable in this dark city of the dead. At last light was seen again, and the Class came out under the blue sky and blazing sunlight.

The ghostly monk pointed back and said: —

"Remember, *there* live the men to whom the Church of God owes her triumphs and her glory! They all died for the faith, and rejoiced to die."

The Class returned to the city, passed the afternoon in visits to the Quirinal Palace, the residence of King Humbert, and the Capuchin

ARCH OF SEPTIMIUS SEVERUS.

Church and its cemetery, which is full of dead monks arranged in ghostly chambers and placed on exhibition like mummies in a museum.

The boys usually obeyed Master Lewis's wishes without questioning them. Almost the only disobedience of the whole journey occurred at Rome.

Master Lewis had requested the Class not to leave the hotel after sundown. But the summer nights were beautiful; the sky was a glory, such as is seldom seen in the regions of the North and West; the streets were gay, and the air cool; and Tommy, on the second evening of the visit said: —

"You will let us go to the Colosseum to-night, will you not, Master Lewis?"

"No, I cannot."

"Why?"

"Because the Roman air on a summer's night is often poisonous to strangers."

"How does it injure them?"

"It produces Roman fever."

On the afternoon of the third day, however, after returning from the Lateran, Tommy proposed to the Class to go out of the city, along the Appian Way, and to visit the remains of the Circus Maxentius.

"We will not return early," he said, "and we will find ourselves belated just about moonrise in the vicinity of the Colosseum."

Wyllys would not consent to go, with this plan to thwart Master Lewis's instructions in view. The other boys, except Charlie, were influenced by Wyllys, and were unwilling to disobey their good teacher by evasion.

"I will go with you," said Charlie. "Master Lewis cannot scold out of me what I may be able to see. Every one who visits Rome goes to see the Colosseum by moonlight."

"When Master Lewis inquires for you," said Wyllys, "where shall we tell him you have gone?"

"To the Circus," said Charlie.

"Tell him we are following the steps of the Apostle Paul," said Tommy.

"I did not know that the Apostle Paul ever went to the Circus," said Wyllys.

"He went over the Appian Way," said Tommy.

About sunset Master Lewis asked Wyllys where were Tommy and Charlie.

"They have gone to walk."

"Where?"

"On the Appian Way."

"How far were they going?"

"To the ruins of the Circus Maxentius."

"Beyond the city? — on the Campagna?" asked Master Lewis, evidently much alarmed. "We had planned to ride over the Appian Way to-morrow. Why did the boys wish to go to-night?"

Wyllys did not reply.

"I shall order a carriage and go after them at once," said Master Lewis.

It was near sunset. The flushed sky threw its mellowed splendors over the desolate Campagna, coloring the long dreary flats, the wastes of ilexes, the barren hillocks, broken monuments, and solitary towers. The Appian Way, with its immense blocks of stone solidly fitted together, was a marvel to Tommy and Charlie, and as they hurried on their wonder grew. The sunset brightened, and Rome became a glory, and the distant hills were like pavilions of light.

"How glorious!" said Charlie.

"I should think so," said Tommy.

"What?"

"Just look back if you want to see a sight to make you marvel."

Charlie looked around.

"Oh!"

VIEW FROM THE PALATINE.

In a queer-looking vehicle driven by a wild-looking man, with small cap, open shirt-bosom, and bare arms, was Master Lewis looking severe and troubled.

"Where are you going?" he asked of Tommy.

"Taking a walk on the Appian Way," said Tommy.

"We are going over the track of the Apostle Paul," said Charlie, who seemed to imagine that so good an aim would partly atone for the disobedience.

"The Apostle Paul did not go in *that* direction," said Master Lewis. "He went the other way — *towards* Rome. You both of you may at once get into the carriage, and *we* will all go towards Rome. And I want you to drive fast," he said to the strange-looking man who held the reins.

The boys looked very disappointed.

"Why did you come after us?" asked Tommy.

"I told you that you must not go about the streets of Rome in the evening; the air is dangerous. But the night air of the city is less likely to produce disease than the atmosphere beyond the walls. Malaria almost depopulates the Campagna, and in summer often turns parts of the city itself into a hospital."

"What is the cause of the malaria?" asked Tommy.

"I cannot tell. It was not so in ancient times. The ways across the Campagna were then lined with houses. There were fine villas in districts now reeking with poison. Pliny says that even the Pontine Marshes, a district long desolated by pestilence, once contained twenty-three cities."

"Do strangers often have the disease?"

"Yes, in summer."

"You were very good to come after us," said Charlie.

"I am sorry I have made you this trouble," said Tommy. "I have disobeyed you but once before."

"The other boys, except Charlie in this instance, have not disobeyed me at all before," said Master Lewis.

Tommy felt the reproof keenly. Charlie's face wore a frightened look. Just as they reached the great spaces — piazzas — within the city, Charlie said, —

"Do you think we shall have the Roman fever?"

"Not if *I* can prevent it," said Master Lewis. "You yourself seem to have done much to give the disease a chance."

Rome is full of statues, villas, piazzas, fountains; hardly in any other city in the world does so much beauty exist out of doors. The restriction against going out in the evening was a hard one for the boys to bear with a very proper spirit, but Master Lewis adhered to it firmly.

There is a fountain in Rome called Trevi; it is one of the most beautiful in the world. There is a legend that if a traveller before leaving the city go to the fountain at night, and take seven sips of the water from a glass, and then break the glass, he will return to Rome again before he dies. The boys tried to persuade Master Lewis to go with them, or permit them to go, to the fountain on the eve of their leaving Rome; but he was not to be influenced by the story of the magic waters to comply with the request.

The evening of the fourth day was spent at the hotel in pleasant conversation. George Howe was to leave the party on the next day and return to Palermo, as he had arranged to take a fruit-boat at that port for New York.

It was agreed to have another informal meeting of the Club on this evening, and to relate stories about the early history of Rome.

Tommy Toby continued the story of the Zigzags of Æneas, and called the narrative, —

FOUNTAIN OF TREVI.

A NEWLY DISCOVERED VERSION OF ÆNEAS AND QUEEN DIDO.

"You were told how Æneas rescued one of the Greeks from Polyphemus at the foot of Mt. Ætna. Soon after this event, as he was sailing away from Sicily in search of the lands which the gods had promised him where he should found a new Troy, a great storm arose, stirred up by Juno, who hated the Trojans, and he was driven to the south, and found shelter in a delightful bay, almost encircled with embowered rocks and cliffs. Here he landed, and the Trojans went into the country in search of food.

"They at last reached the brow of a hill, and to their astonishment saw an unknown race of people building a new and beautiful city. Æneas went to the place and entered the temple, and found its walls adorned with the story of the Siege of Troy.

"I have read this story in some hard lessons in Virgil, very much helped by half-page foot-notes. But I have read a translation of it, published in Connecticut by a youth with modern ideas, that I think is very much more clever and entertaining. It is all so clear that you can understand it without all the while being obliged to refer to the classical dictionary. I shall let this author help me along in my story. Wyllys will hardly appreciate it, his ideas are so old fashioned; but Charlie, who has not read Virgil, will find it very easy to comprehend. There is n't any ambiguity about it.

"Well, Æneas had arrived at Carthage, the new city of Queen Dido. She received him enthusiastically, and asked him to relate to her an account of the Siege of Troy. He told a wonderful story, in which he himself figured as a hero; and Queen Dido, who had resolved never to marry again, became, in spite of her efforts to maintain her purpose, greatly enamored of him. In the language of the poet,—

> "She kept a-thinking what a star was he,
> And how to Heaven he traced his pedigree.
> His reputation as a warryer,
> The conversation that he talked to her,
> His clothes so gorgeous and his style so steep,
> Denied the Queen invigorating sleep."

"'The conversation that he *talked to her*,'" said Charlie; "do you call that a good translation?"

"I call that a *free* translation," said Tommy.

"'His style *so steep*,'" said Charlie. "Virgil never wrote it that way, I know."

"No, but this is a translation one can understand," said Tommy. He continued: —

"Next day the sun rose at the proper time," —

"'*At the proper time*,'" repeated Charlie, in a sarcastic tone.

"Don't interrupt me," said Tommy.

"Next day the sun rose at the proper time,
And much improved the Carthaginian clime;
When thus her sister Anna she addressed:
'Sister, my nights are full of wild unrest.
This nice young man that now is stopping here
To my affections is a-growing dear.
My grief! what savage fights that man has fit,
And how genteel he can get up and git!'"

"'How genteel he can get up and *git*,'" said Charlie. "Go on, it is very interesting."

"I told you so," said Tommy.

"Did she marry him?" asked Charlie.

"I will tell you by and by. He courted her in a most heroic way. You may read all about it in the fourth book of Virgil. But the gods had decreed that he should found a nation in Italy and not at Carthage. So Jupiter sent Mercury to command him to sail away.

"Mercury came to Æneas with the unwelcome message. As the poet says: —

"He faced the Trojan, busy as a bee
Repairing Dido's wash-tub, and says he,
'You drop that hammer like a hot potato,
And put your fleet to sea,'" —

"I don't believe they had potatoes in those days," said Charlie. "But did he go?"

PIAZZA AND GARDEN IN ROME

"Yes, he had to."
"What did Dido do?"
"This is what she did. The poet says:—

> "Completely overcome with woe and passion,
> She fainted in a most *distangay* fashion!
> The screaming maidens bear their prostrate queen
> Unto a bed with tarletan counterpane.
> These read the homeopathy book, while those
> Hold a cologne jar to her pallid nose."

"Did she live?" asked Charlie.
"No; when she saw Æneas sailing away she mounted a funeral pile on the shore—

> "Of seasoned kindling wood, two hundred cords,
> And thus she spoke; these were her latest words:
> 'Behold, I go the way of all mankind!
> I've done the work by changeless fate assigned.'
> With these remarks the deadly dirk she takes
> And in her breast a fatal puncture makes.
> Thrice she supports herself upon her elbow
> And strains her eyes to see her infi*del* beau."

The Class could not repress a smile at this last rhyme, even at this tragic point of the romantic history.

"Well," said Charlie, "and what then?"

> "Then Juno, pitying her agony,
> Sent Iris down the struggling soul to free.
> The dewy Iris, on her saffron wings
> With thousand radiant encolorings,
> Shot through the vapors with immortal speed
> And stood above the death-devoted head.
> 'This lock to Pluto's realms I bear away,
> And now release thee from the ruined clay!'
> So saying, she cut one lock of golden hair,
> And life departed on the sightless air."

"That is fine," said Charlie. "How long will it be, Master Lewis, before I shall be able to read that story in Latin?"

"In the course of a year," said Master Lewis.

"It is a splendid story, is n't it? I wish I could read it now. Can I get a translation of it when I get home?"

"I'll lend you mine," said Tommy.

"The one you have been quoting?"

"Yes."

"I don't want it. I think it is a coarse taste to ridicule a great episode like that. I am resolved to read both Homer and Virgil when I get home; I would rather read them than a story-book."

"Then you can cry in the proper way when you read about Queen Dido. I have cried many a time over Queen Dido," said Tommy.

"When was that?" asked Wyllys.

"When I was compelled to stay after school for not having prepared my translation," said Tommy.

"It is hardly a story to cry over," said George Howe, in his usual practical way. "Queen Dido never saw Æneas. Carthage was not founded until three hundred years after Troy fell. Virgil imagined that 'great episode,' as Charlie calls it. I do not think Greek poetry adds much to one's knowledge in life. I would rather read St. Paul. *There* is philosophy that leads one aright, and harmonizes with what Nature teaches. There was never a Golden Age, and there never will be until all men obey the teachings of the Sermon on the Mount. Life is too short to waste one's thought on things of air."

"You are partly right," said Master Lewis, "but a little too conservative, just as Wyllys is a little too credulous and enthusiastic. St. Paul, whose writings I reverence and read as much as you, himself quoted the Greek poets, as you remember in his discourse on Mars Hill. 'Evil communications corrupt good manners' he says in his Epistle to the Corinthians, which is a quotation from a Greek poet. If it was well for St. Paul, I think it is well for as many as are able, to be familiar with the poets."

"Thank you, Master Lewis," said George frankly. "I never

CALDARIUM OF THE BATHS OF CARACALLA.

thought of the matter in that light. I now remember St. Paul says, 'Add to your faith knowledge,'"—

"'And to knowledge, charity,'" said Master Lewis, kindly.

He added, and his words received the attention of the boys,—

"I love the Greek and the Roman poets, but my mind is not drawn away from the first and essential principles of religion by any human invention or form of art. I believe that there is a single Intelligent Force behind Nature, which planned all things in perfect harmony and will bring perfection out of all things at last; and that that Intelligence is God. I believe that there is a law of right and wrong written in human nature and in the constitution of things,— a law that rewards every virtue and punishes every evil; which always has done so and always will: it is the moral government of God. I believe that our life is a two-fold nature; that the mind which planned the 'Odyssey,' or which sang the Hallelujah Chorus before a note was written, or which frescoed the Sistine Chapel, did not spring from inert dead matter and will not return to dust; but that there is prepared for it a higher life than this.

PRAYER.

"You are in a city in which paganism lies in ruins,— its temples, its altars, its shrines; its poetry only remains. Jesus Christ, in the form of an humble man, came teaching in Galilee. He told the world what virtue was, and how to attain it; what a spiritual life was, and how it was to be sought and found. His teachings were simple truths. Kings tried to crush his gospel; kingdoms to trample it in the dust. His Cross arose, and the temples of paganism began to totter to their ruin. His spiritual kingdom is filling the earth. The pure life he taught, the charity he illustrated, and the spiritual light he promised

PEASANT FAMILY IN ROME.

are the things I most desire; and they are the only things that will last."

The story-telling of the evening was resumed by Mr. Beal, who gave an account of the visit of Æneas to the Cumæan sibyl; but we have not the room for it here.

The Sphinx's Riddle was now inquired for. The boys had not been able to find any satisfactory account of it, so the telling of the story was assigned by Master Lewis to Mr. Beal.

A ROMAN VILLA.

THE SPHINX'S RIDDLE.

Œdipus was the son of Laius and Iocaste, King and Queen of Thebes. Before he was born the Oracle had declared to Laius that he was one day destined to be killed by his own son. When Œdipus came into the world they pierced his feet, whence his name, and carried him to a lonely mountainous place and there left him to perish. He was found there by a shepherd and taken to Corinth, where the king adopted him as his own son, and he was made to believe that the king was really his father.

One day a Corinthian said to him : —

"The king is not your real father."

"I will go to the Oracle at Delphi and see," said the youth.

The Oracle at Delphi made a strange answer to his question : —

"You are destined to slay your own father and to marry your own mother."

Œdipus, thinking the Corinthian king was his father, resolved not to return to Corinth. On the road from Delphi he met a man in a splendid chariot who insulted him. He slew the man. It was Laius, King of Thebes.

About this time there appeared a monster in the vicinity of Thebes, called the Sphinx. She had

THE GERMAN ARTIST.
(See p. 317.)

the face of a woman, the body of a lion, the tail of a serpent, and the wings of a bird. She lived on human beings, and wherever she appeared all the people were filled with terror.

Seated on a rock, she put a riddle to every Theban she saw. If he answered it, he could pass by; if not, she ate him up.

"What was the riddle?" asked Charlie Leland.

"It was this : —

"'*What is that which uses four feet in early life, two feet afterward, and three feet in age, and is the weakest when it uses the most feet?*'"

"What is it?" asked Charlie.

"You must guess."

"Did any one ever guess it?"

"Yes, Œdipus did."

"What did the Sphinx say to him then?"

"She tumbled right off the rock and became a rock herself; and the people were so much pleased with Œdipus that they made him King of Thebes. He married the Queen of Thebes, not knowing that she was his own mother. He at last found out the truth of his parentage, and was led thereby to take his own life."

AN ENTHUSIASTIC COPYIST.
(*See p. 317*)

"But what did Œdipus say to the Sphinx when she asked him the riddle?"

"You must guess."

"I will find a classical dictionary in England, — a comprehensive one; then I will know."

There are more than three hundred churches in Rome, but the only one visited by the Class besides St. Peter's, St. Paul's, and the Lateran was San Pietro in Vinculo, so called for having been erected as a repository of the chains which bound St. Peter in Jerusalem. (Acts xii. 5-7.) Here is seen the majestic statue of Moses, one of the greatest and most wonderful productions of the matchless genius of Michael Angelo. It was originally intended for the monument of

THE MOSES OF MICHAEL ANGELO.

Pope Julius II., who summoned the artist to Rome for the purpose of designing a tomb that should surpass in majesty and magnificence all the other mausoleums in the world. The plan was begun, but never completed."

"Kingly — sublime — terrible!" said Wyllys, standing before the statue.

"Did Moses have *horns?*" asked Charlie.

"Figuratively," said Master Lewis.

"What is the meaning of them?" asked Charlie.

"They represent beams of light, do they not?" said Wyllys, — "the shining of Moses' face when he came down from the mount?"

"In the East," said Master Lewis, "the horn was an ancient emblem of kingly power. People wore horns on their heads as ornaments, and they made them types of royal endowments, as kings wear crowns. The Hebrew Scriptures have many allusions to the custom. The ancients represented the gods as having horns. The artist, in this case, meant to signify that Moses was endowed with vice-regal power by God."

"What is the reclining figure above the statue?" asked Charlie.

"That is Pope Julius."

"And the woman by the side of the Pope, in the niche next to him?"

"That is one of the sibyls," said Master Lewis.

"I must read the history of the sibyls when I return to Boston," said Charlie. "It must be a very wonderful subject. I never heard of the sibyls before I came to Rome; but the figures of Michael Angelo have interested me in them."

We have glanced at the rise of Rome, and had glimpses of her long period of growth and splendor. We must speak also of her fall. When Roman virtue gave place to vicious pleasure, and the Colosseum became the favorite resort of the Court and people, the strength of the queen of empires began to decline. The cup of her iniquities filled, and the time of her downfall and ruin came. The Northern Goths under Alaric, sweeping down from their rugged hills, encompassed her walls, and shut off her supplies. The Romans looked upon the invasion haughtily; but the day of famine came, and women were forced to eat their own children. Then embassadors were sent to the barbaric enemy. They told Alaric that the city would capitulate.

"If you refuse an honorable capitulation," they said, "you may prepare to sound your trumpets, and to give battle to a countless army made furious by despair."

"The thicker the grass the easier it is mowed," replied the Gothic king.

"What will be the price of your retreat from the city?"

"All the gold and all the silver, and every treasure that can be carried away."

"What will you leave us?"

"Your lives."

Alaric departed carrying away with him the treasures that Rome had been gathering for two thousand years. But the city was still beautiful, though her palaces and temples were despoiled.

Soon, however, the Gothic king with his hordes returned. He now stormed the city; he forced the gates, and entered at midnight.

What a scene was there beneath the clouds that darkened the sky! It was like the invasion of an army of fire! The barbarians waved aloft their triumphant torches, and applied them to every temple and palace. Rome became a sea of fire. For six days the sack went on. The young and the old were put to the sword. The city was turned into a tomb, and was destined to remain forever after a museum, a spectacle for all nations to stare at and wonder.

Alaric and his army laden with spoils turned from the blackened city and made a triumphal march along the Appian Way, and left to history the Rome of Romulus, the Consuls, and the Cæsars.

The Gothic conqueror was buried in the bed of a river, which was turned aside from its course to make a place for his tomb. The spoils of the Roman capitol were deposited beside him. Then the river was given its course again, and it flowed over the conqueror and his crowns and treasures forever.

> "My gold and silver ye shall fling
>   Back to the clods that gave them birth, —
> The captured crowns of many a king,
>   The ransoms of a conquered earth:
> For e'en though dead will I control
> The trophies of the capitol.
>
> "Not for myself did I ascend
>   In judgment my triumphal car,
> For God alone on high did send
>   The stern avenger to the war;
> To spread abroad with iron hand
> The appointed scourge of his command.
>
> "Across the everlasting Alp
>   I poured the torrent of my powers,
> And feeble Cæsars shrieked for help
>   In vain within their seven-hilled towers.
> I quenched in blood the brightest gem
> That glittered in their diadem,
> And, lo! the queen of Empires kneels
> And grovels at my chariot wheels!"

The Class had now virtually completed the journey. The boys had taken a view of ancient history in classic lands. The remaining three days in Rome were spent in visits around the city, chiefly outside the walls, where there were many picturesque ruins and beautiful villas.

Tommy visited some of the rooms of the copyists of old masters, and met two enthusiasts in art about whom he told queer stories. One of these was an elegant English gentleman without arms, who was copying a Madonna with his feet; the other was a German artist who ran out his tongue whenever he touched his brush to the canvas on the easel. At another place he saw a Roman family sitting for an artist, the mother making a cradle for her baby in the primitive manner, with her half-recumbent position and outstretched feet.

The city swarmed with beggars, and ignorance and a low moral tone were painfully apparent amid all the splendor, old and new. But the peasants who came into the city from the Campagna often exhibited the old traditional type of Roman beauty, especially the peasant girls with the gracefully folded napkins on their heads, and simple dresses, every part of which showed refinement of taste.

And now, reader, we will part here at Rome. We hope at least that this book will stimulate you to read the many books of history and poetry to which we have referred, and that you may thereby add to the resources of a true and useful life.

www.ingramcontent.com/pod-product-compliance
Lightning Source LLC
Chambersburg PA
CBHW022046230426
43672CB00008B/1083